The Jubilee Memoir Of Queen Victoria

Edward Walford

THE
JUBILEE MEMOIR

OF

HER MAJESTY

QUEEN VICTORIA.

BY

EDWARD WALFORD, M.A.,

Author of the "County Families," &c., &c., &c.

"She wrought her people lasting good."—TENNYSON.

LONDON:

DIPROSE & BATEMAN, SHEFFIELD STREET,

LINCOLN'S INN FIELDS.

1887.

LONDON

DIPROSE, BATEMAN AND CO., PRINTERS,

LINCOLN'S INN FIELDS.

H.R.H. PRINCESS VICTORIA IN HER SEVENTEENTH YEAR (1836).

PREFACE.

I DO NOT think that any word of apology can be necessary for sending out to the public at the present moment a "Jubilee" Memoir of our Most Gracious Queen. At all events, the time is appropriate, and the facts which are here recorded in plain language are such as must come home to the hearts of all her subjects, whether "high or low," whether "rich or poor."

It is right to state here that this little volume is only an expansion of a brief biography of Queen Victoria which I contributed to the *Queen* newspaper in June, 1877, when Her Majesty completed

5

the fortieth year of her reign. Some of the illustrations also have been reproduced from the same source.

Long as her reign has been, that Her Majesty may yet be spared "long to reign over us" is the hearty wish and prayer of, at all events, one of her devoted subjects.

E. W.

Hyde Park Mansions,
              London.
    February, 1887.

CONTENTS.

7

HER MAJESTY
QUEEN VICTORIA.

CHAPTER I.

HER BIRTH AND INFANCY.

She shall be
A pattern to all princes living with her
And all who shall succeed.
SHAKESPEARE, Henry VIII., Act v. Sc. 4.

THE Jubilee of the accession of Queen Victoria to the throne of these realms seems to afford a golden opportunity to the biographer to place upon permanent record the leading events of her life, which has now been extended to her sixty-eighth year. It is too early to pronounce a verdict upon the results of a reign which, long as it has been, bids fair to prove longer

still, and to rival that of her grandfather, King
George the Third, in its duration. We stand too
near to the picture to be able to see, save piecemeal,
that which viewed from the distance which after
years will lend to it, will appear to our eyes as an
harmonious whole; and if there be truth in the
old saying, *nil nisi bonum de mortuis*, there is even
still greater and graver reason from criticising the
actions of a living personage, even if that personage were not our Queen, and the mother of her
people. But whatever length of days may be in
store for Her Majesty, at all events there will be
one prayer to heaven from her loyal subjects,
namely, that her declining years may not be over-
clouded, as his were, by a lingering malady. The
hope and the prayer of one and all amongst us,
from the highest to the lowest, is the long life and
health of the Queen, God bless her!

The only daughter, and indeed the only child of
Edward, Duke of Kent (fourth son of George III.) by
his marriage with the Princess Victoria Mary Louisa;
daughter of His Serene Highness Francis, Duke of
Saxe-Coburg-Saalfeld, and widow of His Serene
Highness Charles Louis Prince of Leiningen, she was
looked on from her birth and earliest infancy as the
possible inheritor of the British Crown; and
accordingly, though her childhood was spent in
the shade of retirement rather than in the sunshine
of public life, she was regarded by her future
subjects with an interest which had not attached

to any member of the Royal Family since the death of her cousin, the Princess Charlotte, in whom so many hopes were centered. The story of her parentage, birth, and childhood, I now proceed to relate.

It will be remembered that the marriage of the Princess Charlotte, the only child of George (Prince of Wales, afterwards George IV.), with Prince Leopold of Belgium, in May, 1816, had been followed in a few short months by her lamented death in childbed, her infant also being born dead. The hopes of the people had been raised high, and their sorrow on learning the sad news was deep in proportion.

> That morn the mighty city silence kept ;
> Grief was upon her, and her spirit wept.

The chasm thus created in the succession to the throne was serious and alarming ; for the people at large, after the long war against the great Napoleon, were not very fond of foreigners, and the old king, George III., had not a single grandchild to inherit his virtues and his throne. In fact, this sad event left the crown without an heir; for of all the numerous family of George III. not one was at that time the parent of a child who, according to the law, could succeed to the throne of these kingdoms. It was, therefore, resolved by the ruling powers—that is, the Prince Regent and his ministers—that it was most important for the interest of the nation at large that the younger sons of the aged king

should form matrimonial alliances with all con-
venient speed, in the hope of an heir being born.
Accordingly, within a few months, the Dukes of
Clarence, Kent and Cambridge, all took to themselves wives from among the daughters of various
German courts, the law of succession to the throne
limiting their choice to Protestants. The lady
selected by the Duke of Kent was her Serene Highness Victoria Mary Louisa, daughter of Francis,
Duke of Saxe-Coburg-Saalfeld, widow of the Prince
of Leiningen, and sister of Prince Leopold of Saxe-
Coburg, afterwards King of the Belgians. The
Prince Edward had been brought up together with
his elder brother, Prince William—afterwards Duke
of Clarence, and ultimately King William IV.—
and on reaching his twenty-first year he had
been created Duke of Kent and Strathearn. He
was early appointed to a military command abroad;
but, owing to his generosity and to serious losses,
he was so far from rich, that he was obliged from
motives of prudence to spend some years at Brussels,
making over to trustees a large annual sum for the
payment of his debts; and it was whilst residing
there that he first met the widowed sister of his
cousin, Prince Leopold.

The Princess— whose first marriage was not a very
happy one by the way—at the time of which we
write was living in seclusion at the Castle of
Amorbach, superintending the education of her
two children, Prince Charles and the Princess

Feodore, aged about twelve and nine years respect-
ively. There were some difficulties to contend with
before the Duke of Kent attained his wish; but,
very soon after the consent of the Prince Regent
had been obtained, the marriage took place—first
according to the Lutheran rite, at Coburg, on May
29, and later in the Anglican Church, on July 11,
1818, at Kew Palace, the Archbishop of Canterbury
officiating, and the Prince Regent himself giving
away the bride.

On their marriage, the Parliament settled an
additional annuity of £6,000 on the Duke of Kent,
with a provision that it should be continued to the
Duchess, in the event of the Duke's death.

After a short stay in England, at Claremont, the
royal pair returned to the continent, and spent the
winter at Amorbach. When, however, there was
good hope of an heir to their house being born, the
Duchess agreed to the patriotic wish of her husband
that the child should be born on English soil. The
Duke was so anxious for the safety of his wife and
his unborn child, that, on the journey to England,
he himself drove the carriage throughout the whole
of the land journey from the Castle of Amorbach
to Kensington Palace, where they arrived early in
April, 1819, accompanied by their daughter, Princess
Feodore. The Duchess was to be seen daily taking
her walk in the garden of the palace till within a
short time of her accouchement, to which her
attendants looked forward with some anxiety. A

KENSINGTON PALACE.

lady, chosen by the Duchess, arrived from abroad to attend on her professionally. Some misgivings of female skill in such cases were felt in England ; but the Duchess of Kent adhered to the custom of the Teutonic matrons, and confided herself to the care of "Dr." Charlotte Siebold. The regular medical attendants were, however, in waiting in case of need.

After a period of suffering, and even of danger for the Duchess, early on the morning of the 24th of May, it was announced to the Ministers and Privy Councillors assembled in an adjoining room, that a Princess was born, and the infant was brought to them by her nurse. Among the distinguished persons who were present were the Dukes of Sussex and Wellington, the Archbishop of Canterbury, Lords Lansdowne and Bathurst, the Bishop cf London, Mr. Canning, and Mr. Nicholas Vansittart, afterwards Lord Bexley. ·The Princess was born at a quarter-past four in the morning ; and the *Gazette* of the same evening announced the fact that "the ycung Princess was in perfect health." The greatest interest was felt by all classes in an event which concerned all from the highest to the lowest ; and it is said that the line of carriages of privileged persons who called to enquire after the Princess and her mother for several days reached from Kensington Palace to Hyde Park Corner.

The nation, which had so lately mourned the

loss of the Princess Charlotte, received with joy the
tidings of the birth of a Princess, the next in
succession to the throne. It was observed at the time,
and it was hailed as a happy omen, that the infant
Princess was born upon the same day which eighty-
one years before had given birth to her grandfather,
though by the change of the old to the new style,
the anniversary was transferred to the 4th of June.

Those who are curious in the matter of Court
gossip may be glad to be told that the bedroom
of the Duchess was on the first floor at the north-
east corner of the palace, and in this room the
future sovereign of these realms was born. Her
nursery, formerly the north drawing room, ad-
joined it.

The baptism of the Princess was not long delayed
after the recovery of her mother. It took place on
the 24th of June, in the grand saloon at Kensington
Palace. Great preparations were made for the ceremony. A contemporary account tells us that "The
superb gold font, kept for the express purpose of
being used for royal christenings, was brought from
the Tower, and the grand saloon was fitted up with
crimson velvet coverings from the Chapel Royal,
at St. James's." The ceremony was performed by
the Archbishop of Canterbury (Dr. Manners Sutton),
assisted by the Bishop of London (Doctor Howley);
and the Princess was named Alexandrina Victoria.
The reason of the choice of these two names is thus
explained by the Hon. Amelia Murray, in her

"Recollections:" " It was believed that the Duke
of Kent wished to name his child Elizabeth, that
being a popular name with the English people.
But the Prince Regent, who was not kind to his
brothers, gave notice that he should stand in person
as one godfather, and that the Emperor of Russia
was to be another. At the baptism, when asked
by the Archbishop of Canterbury to name the
infant, the Prince Regent gave only the name of
'Alexandrina;' but the Duke requested that one
other name might be added, 'Give her her mother's ·
also then; but' he added, 'it cannot precede that
of the Emperor.'" Mr. Charles Greville tells us, in
his " Memoirs and Correspondence," that George
IV. wished the young Princess to be christened
Georgiana. It is to be feared that he was not very
well pleased at finding that he could not have his
own way in the matter. The sponsors of the royal
infant were the Prince Regent, the Emperor Alexander (represented by the Duke of York), the Queen
Dowager of Wurtemberg (represented by the Princess Augusta), and the Duchess Dowager of Coburg
(represented by the Duchess of Gloucester). The
Prince Regent, and, indeed, nearly all the Royal
Family were present at the ceremony, or else at
dinner in the evening. On the following Sunday,
the 27th, in the afternoon, the Duchess of Kent
was publicly churched in the parish church of
Kensington by the Bishop of Salisbury (Dr. John
Fisher).

B

The baptism was registered by the Bishop of London, at the Chapel of St. James's Palace, being signed by the Prince Regent and other notable witnesses. We read in "Queen Victoria," published by Colburn in 1840, on her marriage, that both the baptismal names of the royal lady are united in a beautiful little shrub called the Alexandrine or Victory laurel.

Like a good mother the Duchess of Kent nursed her infant at her own bosom, and always took part personally in dressing and bathing her child, and in all other nursery duties. Indeed for the first ten years of her life the young Princess never slept out of her mother's room.

During the summer the Duke and Duchess, with their infant, were frequently seen by the public during their promenades in the gardens or the environs of Kensington; but on one occasion in July, when the Princess was taken by her parents to a grand review on Hounslow Heath, the Prince Regent expostulated with them, asking, somewhat harshly, why the child was not left at home, as she was too young to be brought into public.

Early in August the Princess was successfully vaccinated; and it appears that she was the first of the Royal Family who received the benefit of this discovery of Jenner. It may interest my lady readers to learn that "at the age of six months the Royal Infant cut her first tooth, and was weaned at the beginning of December." The Duke of Kent was

very fond and proud of his child, and used to express his belief that one day his little "Vic." would
sit on the throne of England.

It so happened that the autumn was chilly, and
the cold weather set in early this year; and in order
to enjoy a warmer climate, and to escape the London fogs, the Duke and Duchess made choice of
Sidmouth as a residence for the winter. On the
way thither with the Princess they paid a visit to
the Bishop of Salisbury, who had been tutor to the
lamented Princess Charlotte. Woolbrook Cottage,
the residence of General Baynes, in a beautiful
situation outside Sidmouth, was taken by the Duke;
and the Royal party arrived there on Christmas
Eve. Such was the slowness of travelling, owing
to the badness of the roads, that the journey from
Salisbury to Sidmouth took nearly two days, and
the Royal party were obliged to break it by spending the night at an inn at Ilminster.

They were received with every token of joy by
the residents of Sidmouth : but only a few short
weeks of domestic happiness awaited them there;
and those weeks were passed in quiet home plea-
sures. One incident occurred, which providentially
caused only a moment's alarm ; for a boy, who was
shooting small birds, was so near the cottage that a
shot broke the window of the nursery and passed
close to the head of the infant Princess. It would
seem therefore that from her cradle Victoria carried about with her a "charmed life."

The illness of the Duke, which so soon carried
him off from the joys of home, was caused, it is
believed, by neglect.   He had got his feet wet
during a long walk; but he delayed changing his
boots till after he had received some visitors and
had spent some time with his little daughter, who
by her smiles had drawn him to play with her.
He caught a violent cold, and it was not long before
inflammation attacked his chest, and fever set in.
Doctors were summoned from London; but, notwithstanding all that was done, he expired about ten
days after the attack, early on the morning of Sunday, January 23rd, 182c Thus, within the space of
little more than a month, Woolbrook Cottage was
suddenly changed from a scene of joy and happiness,
into a chamber of sorrow and death.   The Duchess
had kept anxious and willing watch by his bedside for
five successive nights.   Her brother, Prince Leopold,
who arrived on the last day of the Duke's life,
proved a great comfort to his sister, He accompanied the widow and infant Princess on their
return journey to Kensington, where they arrived
after another stay at the palace at Salisbury.   It so
happened, that on the very day of their return to
Kensington, the Princess's grandfather, George III.,
expired; and a few days later his remains, and
those of her father, were consigned to the royal
vaults, beneath St. George's Chapel, at Windsor.*

---

* Her Majesty, many years afterwards, erected a handsome painted
window in the parish church at Sidmouth, as a memorial to her illustrious
father.

Owing to the liberality of his sentiments and to his genial manners, the Duke was extremely popular with the nation, and his sudden death was felt as a national loss.

As a proof of the religious feelings of the Queen's father, I may be allowed here to quote, from the "Life of the Duke of Kent," the following anecdote, related by a clergyman who was often admitted to his presence:

"Two or three evenings previous to his visit to Sidmouth I was at Kensington Palace; and on my rising to take leave, the Duke intimated his wish that I should see the infant Princess in her crib, adding, 'As it may be some time before we meet again, I should like you to see the child, and give her your blessing.' The Duke preceded me into the little Princess's room, and on my closing a short prayer, that as she grew in years she might grow in grace, and favour both with God and man, nothing could exceed the fervour and feeling with which he responded in an emphatic 'Amen.' Then with no slight emotion he continued, 'Don't pray simply that her's may be a brilliant career, and exempt from those trials and struggles which have pursued her father; but pray that God's blessing may rest on her, that it may overshadow her and that in all her coming years she may be guided and guarded by God.' That prayer was offered."

PRINCESS VICTORIA AT ABOUT SIX YEARS OF AGE.

CHAPTER II.

HER EARLY CHILDHOOD.

See! in the sunshine of a mother's smile,
  Under the mantle of a mother's care,
A maid, the hope of England, blooms awhile,
  Bright as the jewel in Aurora's hair,
  Fresh as the rose, and as the lily fair;
Whom with enduring virtue heaven endow
  The burden of a kingly crown to bear.

HE above lines I have ventured to prefix to this chapter as most apposite to my subject, though I know not their author's name.

An interesting proof that the Princess Victoria, young as she was, had not forgotten her father, was afforded by the fact that, on the Duke of York first coming to Kensington to offer his condolence to his widowed sister-in-law, his niece put out her arms to him with the same symptoms of joy as she was used to show when she saw her father. She

showed the same infantine intelligence a few weeks
afterwards on seeing his bust in marble. The
Duke was touched by this, it is said, and he
promised to be a father to her. The Princess
repaid his love, and in his last illness, we learn
from "An Anecdotal Memoir of the Queen," she
"visited him daily, always carrying in her hand a
bouquet of choice flowers."

Addresses of condolence on her bereavement
were presented by both Houses of Parliament to
the Duchess of Kent, who received them with her
child in her arms. These addresses were presented
on Monday, the 21st of February, and the representatives of various charitable institutions which
the Duke had supported, were not slow in following
suit. It is needless to add that all of them met
with most gracious replies.

Even when little more than an infant, the
Princess showed marked signs of intelligence, and
whenever she was presented with a new toy, she
never forgot to recognise the giver when next she
saw the donor. She is thus described by the
author of "An Anecdotal Memoir of the Queen,"
who used often to see her in Kensington Gardens:

"She was at this period a beautiful child, bearing
a very strong resemblance to her father, and indeed
to the Royal Family generally. Though small and
delicately formed, she was very fat, and might be
called a remarkably fine child for her age; her eyes
were large and blue, her complexion extremely fair,

with a rosy colour, expressive of high health, and her curled lips, continually parted, showed her four pretty white teeth. She was forward in her speech, very lively, and apparently of a gentle, happy temper, occasionally a sweet and merry smile animated her intelligent countenance. She was dressed in a white cambric pelisse neatly frilled at the bottom, and a large straw bonnet, trimmed with black ribbons. We were informed by her nurse that she did not yet run alone, indeed she was not entirely short-coated until more than a year old; doubtless in order to prevent her from being placed upon her feet too early."

It appears that many of those who saw the child noticed in her a great resemblance to the late Princess Charlotte; and they, perhaps, on this account all the more readily transferred their affection to their new "fair-haired daughter of the Isle." On the first anniversary of her birth the Princess (wearing a black sash over her simple dress) received visits from her relatives, and she soon began to "lisp her first words," and was taught to greet the portraits and busts of her father with the word "papa." "Her large blue eyes, beautiful bloom, and fair complexion," we are told, "made her already a model of infantine beauty."

William Wilberforce, the friend of the slaves, writing to his friend, Mrs. Hannah More, thus mentions the scene in the drawing room at Kensington :—" In consequence of a very civil message

from the Duchess of Kent, I waited on her this
morning. She received me with her fine animated
child on the floor by her side with its playthings,
of which I soon became one. . . . She apolo-
gised for not speaking English well enough to talk
it ; but intimated 'a hope that she might speak it
better and longer with me at some future time."

At the end of 1820 a daughter was born to the
Duke of Clarence : this child, had she lived, would
have succeeded to the Crown, but she died in infancy.
Still, as there was a possibility of other children
being born to the Duke of Clarence, the Princess
Victoria was brought up in comparative seclusion,
and the prospect of the high destiny to which she
might possibly one day be called was rather kept from
her, for after all she was only presumptive heiress
to the throne. The Duchess of Kent, who had been
left sole guardian of her daughter, soon gained the
esteem of the nation. Her own words will best
describe her situation at this time : "A few months
after the birth of my child," she said, " my infant
and myself were awfully deprived of father and
husband. We stood alone, almost friendless and
unknown in this country. I could not even speak
its language. I did not hesitate how to act. I gave
up my home, my kindred, and other duties to devote
myself to a duty which was to be the sole object of
my future life."

The life of the Duchess and her children at
Kensington was plain and simple. The family

party met at breakfast at eight o'clock in summer time, the Princess Victoria having her bread and milk and fruit put on a little table by her mother's side.   After breakfast the Princess Feodore studied with her governess, Miss Lehzen, and the Princess Victoria went out for an hour's walk or drive. From ten to twelve her mother instructed her; after which she would amuse herself by running through the suite of rooms which extended round two sides of the palace, and in which were many of her toys.   Her nurse was a Mrs. Brock, whom the Princess used to call her "dear, dear Boppy."   At two came a plain dinner, while the Duchess took her luncheon.   After this, lessons again till four; then would come a visit or drive, and after that the Princess would ride or walk in the gardens, or occasionally on very fine evenings the whole party would sit out on the lawn under the trees.   At the time of her mother's dinner the Princess had her supper laid at her side; then, after playing with her nurse, she would join the party at dessert, and at nine she would retire to her bed, which was placed by the side of her mother's.   In fact, during the whole of her infancy the little Princess was a familiar presence in the gardens of Kensington Palace, where she gained health and strength by running about freely and without restraint or ceremony, and where she was taught to return with civility the friendly greetings of all persons whom she met.

With reference to the usual outdoor exercise of
the Princess during her childhood, I am sure that
my lady readers will be pleased if I introduce the
following remarks, which were sent to the editor
of a daily paper when the Princess was nearly three
years old :—

"Passing accidentally through Kensington Gardens, a few days since, I observed at some distance
a party, consisting of several ladies, a young child,
and two men-servants, having in charge a donkey,
gaily caparisoned with blue ribbons, and accoutred
for the use of the infant. The appearance of the
party, and the general attention they attracted, led
me to suspect they might be the royal inhabitants
of the palace. I soon learnt that my conjectures
were well founded, and that Her Royal Highness
the Duchess of Kent was in maternal attendance,
as is her daily custom upon her august and interesting daughter, in the enjoyment of her healthful
exercise. On approaching the royal party, the
infant Princess, observing my respectful recognition,
nodded, and wished me a 'good morning,' with much
liveliness, as she skipped along between her mother
and her sister, the Princess Feodore, holding a hand
of each. Having passed on some paces, I stood a
moment to observe the actions of the child, and
was pleased to see that the notice with which she
honoured me was extended, in a greater or less
degree, to almost every person she met. Her Royal
Highness is remarkably beautiful, and her gay and

animated countenance bespeaks perfect health and
good temper. Her complexion is excessively fair,
her eyes large and expressive, and her cheeks
blooming. She bears a very striking resemblance
to her late royal father, and indeed to every member
of our reigning family. But the soft beauty and,
if I may be allowed the the term, the dignity of
her infantine countenance, peculiarly reminded me
of her cousin, our late beloved Princess Charlotte."

" This favourite donkey," we are further told by
the same authority, " was a present from the Duke
of York, and bore his Royal mistress daily through
the gardens to her great delight, so fond, indeed,
was she of him, and of the exercise which he procured for her, that it generally was found necessary
to persuade her that the donkey was tired or hungry,
in order to induce her to alight."* Even at
that very early age, the Princess took great
pleasure in mixing with the people generally, and
seldom passed anybody in the gardens, either when
riding in her little carriage or upon her donkey,
without accosting them with, " How do you do ? "
or " Good-morning, sir," or " lady " and she always
seemed pleased to enter into conversation with
strangers, returning their compliments or answering
their questions in the most distinct and good-
humoured manner. The young Princess showed
her womanly nature as a particular admirer of

---

* As we proceed further, we shall find other instances of Queen Victoria's
fondness for animals, and tenderness towards them.

children, and rarely allowed an infant to pass her,
without requesting permission to inspect it and to
take it in her arms. She expressed great delight at
meeting a young ladies' school, and always had
something to say to most of the children, but particularly to the younger ones. When a little older,
she was remarkable for her activity, as, holding her
sister Feodore in one hand, and the string of her
little cart in the other, with a moss rose fastened
into her bosom, she would run with astonishing
rapidity the whole length of the broad gravel walk,
or up and down the green glades with which the
gardens abound, her eyes sparkling with animation
and glee, until the attendants, fearful of the effects
of such violent exercise, were compelled to put a
stop to it, much against the will of the little romp;
and although a large assemblage of well-dressed
ladies, gentlemen, and children, would, on such
occasions, form a semicircle round the scene of
amusement, their presence never seemed in any way
to disconcert the royal child, who would continue
her play, occasionally speaking to the spectators as
though they were partakers in her enjoyment,
which, in very truth, they were. If, whilst amusing
herself in the enclosed lawn, she observed, as sometimes happened, many persons collected round the
green railings, she would walk close up to it, and
curtsey and kiss her hand to the people, speaking
to all who addressed her; and when her nurse led
her away, she would again and again slip from her

hand, and return to renew the mutual greetings
between herself and her future subjects, who, as
they contemplated with delight her bounding step
and merry healthful countenance, the index of a
heart full of innocence and joy, were ready unani-
mously to exclaim : —

> " Long may it be ere royal state
>   That cherub smile shall dissipate ;
>   Long ere that bright eye's peerless blue,
>   A sovereign's anxious tear bedew ;
>   Ere that fair form of airy grace,
>   Assume the regal measured pace ;
>   Or that young, open, cloudless brow,
>   With truth and joy that glitters now,
>   The imperial diadem shall wear
>   Beset with trouble, grief, and care."

The Princess, to speak the truth, was from the
first, rather self-willed, and showed much independence and individuality of character; but her
education was carried on with regularity and with
very great success. She was a favourite of those
who taught her. She speedily became proficient
in three languages (English, German, and French);
and we are told that " she often begged little favours
of her mother in German, though she was most
familiar with her native tongue." But it was not
in books only that she was taught, her education
was practical; she was taught from her earliest
years the value of industry and good habits; and
if in after life the child showed that she possessed

those qualities in an eminent degree, she knew and
acknowledged that they were the outcome of her
mother's training.

In 1822, when the Princess was just three years
of age, she nearly met her death in Kensington
Gardens. A soldier, named John Maloney, was
the happy instrument of saving her, and I use his
own words. "I happened to be in Kensington
gardens, when my attention was taken by a pony-
carriage, in which was seated a child; the pony was
superbly harnessed, and was led by the page, who
walked at its head with the rein in his hand.
A lady walked on one side of the carriage and a
young woman walked behind. I admired the pony
and walked close after or behind the page, when
suddenly a large dog came from the water with a
stick crossways in its mouth, and ran under the
pony's forelegs, causing it to plunge, bringing the
wheels of one side of the carriage on to the foot-
way, and turning it over, the child being thrown
out head downwards, and would have been crushed
under the carriage, but I grasped her dress and
swung her into my arms before she came to the
ground, but in doing so, I brought her instep
against the step of the carriage, by which she
received a slight wound." Malony also received a
slight wound on the thigh. The crowd which
assembled made a collection for him on the spot,
and he received also a golden guinea from the lady
who was with the carriage. About four years

later, he was presented with £5 from the Duchess of Kent, with a promise of being advanced in the service. It is to be hoped that the promise was kept; for Malony certainly seems to have saved the flower of England from an early tomb.

On her fourth birthday George IV. presented to his niece a very handsome miniature portrait of himself, set in diamonds; and soon after this the Princess was taken, at His Majesty's special request, to Carlton House, on the occasion of a state banquet, that he might renew his acquaintance with her, not having seen her since she was a year old, and also present her to his guests. The King was pleased with his little niece, and from this time felt as much affection for and interest in her as was possible for a man of his habits and tastes. The Princess, we are told, full of childish glee in joyful anticipation of this memorable visit, cried out, "am I going really to see the King?" Then turning to her mother, she asked "Oh! mamma, shall I go upon my donkey?" This donkey, it should be here explained, was a present from her uncle, the Duke of York, and at that time the greatest treasure that she possessed in the world, and one which, as the King had never seen it, she thought would please His Majesty. On this occasion it is recorded that the Princess appeared simply dressed in a plain white frock, the short sleeve of her left arm being looped up and fastened with her uncle's beautiful birthday gift.

C

It was about this time thought proper by His Majesty that funds should be provided for the education and establishment of the Princess, for whom Prince Leopold, like a good and kind uncle, had hitherto handsomely found the expenses; and a message was accordingly sent to Parliament, requesting that the country should contribute an adequate sum—the £6,000 income which had been settled on the Duchess having been made without any reference to possible issue. Another sum of £6,000 annually was accordingly voted by Parliament for the maintenance of the Princess, and in both Houses the Duchess was spoken of in terms of high praise for the devoted care which she showed in bringing up her daughter. In the Upper House of Parliament Lord Liverpool said: "I have had opportunities of observing the conduct of the Duchess of Kent, which is unexampled for propriety, domestic affection, and moral purity."

The seventh birthday of the Princess was kept by the desire of her uncle, Prince Leopold, at Claremont, where there was a *fête* and a procession of her dolls, fifteen in number, each named after some one or other of her royal relatives, and all dressed by the Princess herself, with the aid of her nurse, Mrs. Brock. Among the presents on this occasion was a pair of tiny mouse-coloured ponies brought from the Scottish Highlands, by Lady Huntly, afterwards Duchess of Gordon. A portrait of the Princess driving out with this Lilliputian equipage was drawn on stone by Doyle, and published by Dickenson, of Bond Street.

The Princess Victoria, from her position and possible prospects, was naturally surrounded by much courtly etiquette; and, as the Princess Feodore was so many years older than herself, and of course, therefore, not much of a companion 'for her, she felt deeply the want of a playmate. A proof of this fact was afforded when a musical prodigy, five years old, named Lyra, was brought in to amuse the Princess at Kensington Palace by her wonderful performance on the harp. While the child was playing a beautiful air, with which the Princess appeared to be entirely taken up, as she had great taste for music, the Duchess left the room ; but on her return she found the Princess and the child-musician seated on the hearthrug, and looking at the former's toys, some of which the Princess was offering to the child.

Before the Princess had attained her fifth year, her regular education was commenced, under the superintendence of the Rev. George Davys, after-wards Dean of Chester and Bishop of Peterborough. It is said that he found that his royal pupil had a strong will of her own, though she proved herself in a short time to be docile and apt, and made great progress in her studies, perhaps all the more keen because she had never been forced to learn out of books ; the Duchess of Coburg, her grandmother, having strongly advised the Duchess of Kent " not

to tease her little puss with learning whilst she was
so young."

The Princess paid several visits in these early
years to the King at Windsor, by whom she was
treated with every indulgence, and also to Prince
Leopold, at his quiet seat at Claremont, where she
spent several weeks at a time. At this latter place
her taste for flowers was increased by her uncle,
who instructed her in botany, a favourite science
of his own, and also encouraged her in sketching
from nature, an art in which, even as a child, she
showed a considerable taste and skill.

The Duke of York, who was the favourite uncle
of the Princess, died when she was in her eighth
year; and the Princess felt keenly the loss which
brought her a step nearer to the throne, though it
is believed that up to this time she had hardly any
idea of the high destiny which in all probability
awaited her.

When the Princess Feodore was eighteen years
of age, her governess, Mademoiselle Lehzen, transferred her services to the Princess Victoria; a very
good proof that she had been successful in helping
to form the mind of her first charge; and while
Dr. Davys superintended the more solid part of
her education, her governess had the care of the
lighter parts, which included lessons in music by
Mr. J. B. Sale (at the special request of George IV.),
and in dancing by Madame Bourdin; while Mr.
Steward, the writing-master at Westminster School,

gave her instructions in writing and arithmetic.
That his royal pupil profited by Mr. Stewart's
instructions will be clear to those who notice the
boldness and freedom of the Queen's autograph
signature, written shortly after her accession to the
throne.

At about the age of nine the Princess had her
first introduction to the sight of a Court Drawing
Room, at which it happened that the young Queen
of Portugal was present. She first danced in public
at a juvenile ball, to which the King invited her
in order to meet the young Queen, to whose brilliant
robes and surroundings the young Princess offered
a striking contrast by the simplicity of her dress
and manners. On that occasion (we are told by
the Court chronicler) the Princess danced with
the young Lord Fitzalan, the heir of the Howards,
and also with Prince William of Saxe-Weimar, the
Prince Esterhazy, and the sons of the Earls of

Delawarr and Jersey. The Princess, we are told, even at this early age, evidently had a great taste for Court life, for we are told that she often amused herself by dressing her dolls in Court costume, and by rehearsing the programme of miniature receptions at Court.

CHAPTER III.

HER GIRLHOOD.

This Royal Infant (Heaven still move about her),
Though in the cradle, yet now promises
Upon this land, a thousand, thousand blessings,
Which time shall bring to ripeness.

SHAKESPEARE, Henry VIII., Act v., Sc. 4.

AFTER the Princess had passed from the nursery into the school-room, the autumn months were usually passed by herself and the Duchess of Kent, at one or other of the bathing-places on the coast of Kent or Sussex, and there it was that the former first imbibed that love for the sea which constantly crops up in her diary, and which has never left her.

Broadstairs was one of the first places selected by the Duchess of Kent, though Ramsgate became their favourite resort, as Prince Leopold

had a residence there. Their residence at Ramsgate
was Towneley House, overlooking the harbour.
They were also occasional residents during the
autumn at Tunbridge Wells, where they occupied
Calverley House, and at St. Leonards-on-Sea,
where they rented a house on the Marina. A considerable part of the summer and autumn of 1833
was spent by the Princess and her mother at
Norris Castle, near East Cowes. From this place
they made excursions to Carisbrooke Castle, to
Southampton (where they were present at the
opening of the new landing pier), to Portsmouth,
Swanage, Weymouth, Lyme Regis, Exeter, Torquay,
Devonport and Plymouth, performing part of this
latter expedition by land, and partly in the royal
yacht. At Plymouth the Princess presented the
89th Royals with a new stand of colours, and made
an excursion to the Eddystone lighthouse. At
Plymouth the Princess narrowly escaped a terrible
accident; for the royal yacht came into collision
with another vessel with such a shock that her sail
and gaff fell on the deck where she was standing.
A sailor sprang forward, caught the Princess in
his arms, and rescued her from the peril — a
moment more, and perhaps the Crown of England
would have passed in another direction. Her pre-
server, it need not be added, was liberally rewarded
for his service. Wherever they went their visits
were hailed with pleasure by rich and poor alike.
Their quiet and unostentatious manners, their

mingling with the people on the sands and promenades, and the many little acts of charity recorded
to their credit, made a pleasant and a lasting impression on their neighbours, and on all with whom
they were brought into personal contact.

We have said that the Queen probably had a
very slight idea of the station to which she would,
while yet in her early years, be called; and it is
believed that it was during her study of English
history with her governess, when about eleven
years of age, that her attention was first seriously
drawn to some point in connection with the succession to the Crown.   After thinking for a few
moments, she inquired who would be the presumptive heir in the case of the death of the King.
To the reply that she had several uncles, she
observed that her own papa came next to the Duke
of Clarence, and that it appeared to her, from what
she had just been reading, that when both he and
the present King passed away, she herself would be
the successor to the throne.   As this could not be
denied, the occasion was turned to account by the
governess impressing upon her pupil the importance
of endeavouring to make use of all the means intended to form her mind, so as " to render herself
not unworthy of so high a possible destiny."

On the death of King George IV. in 1830, the
Duke of Clarence ascended the throne as William
IV.; and thus, as the duke had no children, the
Princess Victoria stood next in direct succession to

the Crown. She was accordingly, from this time, brought out in a great measure from her life of comparative retirement.

Though she was not present at the coronation of King William, being with her mother in the Isle of Wight (a circumstance which gave rise to no little gossip at the time), she appeared at the first review held soon afterwards by the King in Hyde Park, in company with her mother and Queen Adelaide; and she stood at the side of her uncle when he held his first Chapter of the Order of the Garter. She also appeared at Court at the first Drawing Room held by the new Queen. She was also present at the meeting of the new Parliament; and in the early days of 1831 she was seen for the first time at a theatre, when the pantomime was performed at Covent Garden.

In the autumn of 1831 the Duchess of Kent went with her daughter for a tour through some of the midland counties, and settled for a time at Malvern, where the Princess was often seen in full enjoyment of the invigorating air of the hills. They visited Birmingham, and inspected some of its principal manufactures. They drove over to see Worcester Cathedral, for the Princess took a special interest in architecture and church music. They were also entertained at Eastnor Castle and Madresfield Court, both in the neighbourhood of Malvern, the seats of Lords Somers and Beauchamp. In 1832 they made acquaintance with some of the

beauties of North Wales ; and after passing through
Coventry and Shrewsbury they visited Powis
Castle, Wynnstay, and Beaumaris, where the Princess was present at the "Eisteddfodd" of North
Wales. They also visited the gallant general, Lord
Anglesey, at Plas Newydd, his seat in Anglesea,
and on the return journey spent a day at Eaton
Hall with the Marquis of Westminster, and another
at Oakley Park, near Ludlow, with the Clives, who
were near relatives of the Duchess of Northumberland. On their homeward route the Princess and
her mother stayed a day or two at Chester, to inspect its cathedral ; and paid visits to several of the
nobility *en route*, seeing Chatsworth, the princely
seat of the Cavendishes, Hardwicke Hall, Shug-
borough Hall, the seat of Lord Lichfield, and Alton
Towers, that of Lord Shrewsbury. From the latter
seat they went to see Lichfield Cathedral, and admired Chantrey's exquisite sculpture of "The
Sleeping Children." They also paid visits to Lords
Liverpool, Plymouth, and Abingdon. From Wytham
Abbey, the seat of the last-named nobleman, they
drove over to see Oxford ; and it is needless to add
that their welcome by the authorities of the University in the Theatre was most enthusiastic, as became
that most loyal seat of learning. During the next
summer several excursions were made by them in
the "Emerald" yacht, from Norris Castle, in the Isle
of Wight ; and the Princess took great interest in
all affairs relating to the sea in the course of her

visits to Torquay, Plymouth, and the Eddystone
Lighthouse—places with which she afterwards renewed her acquaintance in the course of her yachting tours in company with the Prince Consort.

In July of the year 1834, the Princess was confirmed by the Archbishop of Canterbury at the
Chapel Royal, and on the Sunday following she
received her first Communion in the private chapel
of Kensington Palace. During the autumn, after
a visit to Tunbridge Wells, the Princess and her
mother made a tour through several parts of the
North of England, visiting the Earls of Harewood
and Fitzwilliam, the Archbishop of York, and the
Duke of Rutland, who entertained the royal party
at Belvoir. From Bishopsthorpe they went to the
great musical festival at York Minster; and they
were present at the Doncaster races. On their
way back to London they paid visits to Lord
Exeter at Burleigh, "Burleigh House, by Stamford
town," and the Duke of Grafton, at Euston Hall.
They were heartily welcomed wherever they
appeared, especially at Wisbech and Lynn, where
their horses were taken out of the carriage, in
order that the Princess Victoria's future subjects
might be able to boast that they had drawn her
through the streets with their own hands. Later in
the year they spent some time at Ramsgate, and
passed a few days with the Duke of Wellington at
Walmer Castle.

During their stay at Tunbridge Wells in 1834,

the Princess and her mother walked daily on the Parade and on the Common, attended the races, fancy fairs, horticultural shows, &c.; and before leaving the Princess performed her first public act by laying the first stone of some new schools in the Calverley Park, which were named after her. The august party also visited Knowle, Penshurst, Eridge, and the other neighbouring noblemen's seats, including Buckhurst Park, where they were present at Lord Delawarr's annual dinner to his peasantry.

About this time her tutor, Dr. Davys, was made Dean of Chester, and the Duchess of Northumberland undertook the duties of state governess to the Princess, Mdlle. (afterwards Baroness) Lehzen still superintending her general studies.

As Prince Leopold had shown so deep an interest in his niece, and taken so large a part in providing for her education, we may remind our readers that at about this time he was called by the powers to the throne of Belgium. He was still, however, constant in his visits to England, and afforded his sister and his niece every aid in his power, in the way of counsel and advice, during the rest of his life.

In the first Parliament of William IV., the Duchess of Kent was formally appointed Regent of the kingdom, in the possible event of her daughter ascending the throne before she should have attained her legal majority—a strong proof of the confidence which the nation felt in the Duchess personally. This fact, though it is not generally known, ought not to be forgotten, as redounding greatly to her credit as a woman and a mother.

On Prince Leopold's acceptance of the crown of Belgium, and his voluntary relinquishment, in consequence, of his annuity as widower of Princess Charlotte, the King sent a message to Parliament, requesting that a more suitable provision should be made for the Duchess of Kent, and for the education and support of the Princess, her daughter; and it was accordingly agreed that £10,000 per annum should be added to the £6,000 which had been voted previously.

From this time forward, Claremont, which had been given up by Prince Leopold as a residence, became the favourite abode of the Princess Victoria, who spent many of the happiest days of her childhood within its walls, roaming through its gardens and shrubberies, free from the restraints of Kensington Palace.

Among the treasures of Claremont are several portraits of the Princess Victoria in her childhood, including one by Sir William Beechey; and a snuff box presented by the Princess Charlotte to Prince Leopold, with the following inscription :—

See Claremont's terrac'd heights and Esher's groves,
Where in the sweetest solitude, embraced
By the soft windings of the silent Mole,
From Courts and Cities Charlotte finds repose.
Enchanting vale ! beyond whate'er the Muse
Has of Achaia or Hesperia sung ;
A vale of bliss !

The above lines are from the pen of Thomson in his "Seasons," and as the name of "Charlotte" has been substituted for that of "Pelham," so there can be little doubt that the name of "Victoria" might be inserted in its place with equal truth.

Claremont was built by Vanbrugh, but was soon afterwards bought by Holles, Earl of Clare (afterwards Duke of Newcastle), who named it after himself. The gardens, shrubberies, etc., were laid out by Kent, the landscape gardener. It became afterwards, the residence of the great Lord Clive, to whom an obelisk is erected in the grounds. Having passed through some intermediate hands, it was bought in 1816 for Prince Leopold and the Princess Charlotte, who spent here the few short months of her married life, and who died here as already mentioned. The place is a sort of "mausoleum to the Princess," and its memories are sad enough; yet we hear from "Our Home in the Highlands" that it was the favourite home of the Princess Victoria's childhood and girlhood, and that she first learned in its pleasant glades to sketch from nature—an art which she cultivated in her after life with much success. The pleasure grounds occupy about sixty acres, but the rest of the estate is occupied by long avenues of beeches, oaks, and elms, firs, pines and cedars and a lake.

"Claremont," Queen Victoria writes to her uncle Leopold, in January, 1843, "has a peculiar charm for us both; and to me it brings back recollections of the happiest days of my otherwise dull childhood when I experienced from you, my dearest uncle, that kindness which has ever since continued . . . . . Victoria* plays now with my old bricks, etc., and I see her running and jumping in the flower garden, much as *old*, though, I fear, still little, Victoria of former days used to do."

It is well known that Her Majesty is (or at all events, was) an accomplished horsewoman; and it was at this period that she took her first lessons in riding from Mr. Fozard, an able professor, who was, like most of her other instructors, remembered by his pupil in later life. In her studies the Princess had by this time made great progress; she spoke French and German fluently, and was familiar with Italian. We are told that she read Virgil and Horace, and had even begun Greek; for mathematics she showed great taste, as also for music and drawing.

The Princess, even when she was quite young, was passionately fond of music and the opera; and it is recorded in one of the newspapers in 1838, that, although she rarely went to the theatres, Her Majesty had attended the Opera House thirty-three nights out of thirty-nine, the exceptions being compulsory on account of assemblies at Buckingham Palace. But I am anticipating events.

In June, 1835, the Princess was seen for the first

---

* The Princess Royal, now Princess Imperial of Germany.

time with the Court at Ascot races, which, after
her accession, she generally honoured with her presence on the Gold Cup Day up to the period of
her great bereavement.

Of the young Princess Victoria, before she had
assumed the burdens of royalty Sir John Hobhouse
gives a pleasing sketch in his Diary and Memoirs.
Dining at Kensington Palace with the Duchess of
Kent, he tells us that he sat next to the Princess,
who was seated at her mother's right hand: " The
young Princess," he writes, "was treated in every
respect like a grown-up woman, although apparently quite a child.   Her manners were very pleasing and natural, and she seemed much amused by
some conversation with Lord Durham, a manifest
favourite at Kensington.   When she left the room
she curtsied round very prettily to all the guests
who were present, and then ran out of the
room."

Sir John Hobhouse then very naturally goes on
to ask, " What will become of this young, pretty,
unaffected child in a few, few years ? "   The
answer to his query was written many years afterwards. Seldom, if ever, has it been possible to
answer a similar question more satisfactorily. I
quote what may be called a personal comment, not
being able to give the answer at length: "An interval of thirty-three years, a reign of twenty-eight
years—some of them in very difficult, if not dan-
gerous, times—and the greatest of all calamities

D

that can befall a woman and a Queen, have not
deprived her of the smile, the kind and gracious
smile, which charmed me in those long bygone
days, and with which she received an old servant
and subject only two days ago."

On the 24th of May, 1837, the Princess Victoria
attained her eighteenth year, and her legal majority
was celebrated with great rejoicings. We need
scarcely remind our readers that all royal personages are held to be of age three years before their
subjects. On this occasion we are told that a
musical *matineé* was held under the windows of the
Princess at Kensington Palace in the early morning,
thirty-seven vocal and instrumental performers
taking part in it. The day was kept as a general
holiday at Kensington, where flags waved from the
church tower, and from almost every window and
balcony along the High Street. It is not a little
singular, if indeed it is true, that among the first
to congratulate the Princess upon the happy event
was her cousin, Prince Albert of Saxe-Coburg.
The King made a present of a very fine piano to
his niece on the occasion; a grand ball also was
given in her honour at St. James's Palace (at which
for the first time the Princess took precedence of
her mother), and very many addresses of congratulation poured in upon her. The illuminations also
were very general, both in the City and at the
West End. The King and Queen were absent
from this ball on account of the indisposition of the

former; and during the next day the King's illness considerably increased; indeed, upon the very day of his niece's majority may be said to have commenced the attack which shortly afterwards caused the demise of the Crown.

We learn incidentally from Mr. Raikes' "Journal" that on the Princess Victoria coming of age, it was proposed by her uncle, the King, to form for her an establishment of her own; but that the suggestion was " combated by her mother, as it would have given the nomination of the appointments to the then Court party." The death of King William, however, which happened very shortly afterwards, put an end to the idea.

It was a pretty trait in the character of the youthful Princess that, when at this time King William expressed his wish to increase her income, the former, knowing the distressed state of the public revenue, would not consent to an application to Parliament on the subject, and was with difficulty brought to accept an extra £10,000 a year in order to bestow on charities befitting her station.

CHAPTER IV.

HER ACCESSION AND CORONATION.

"O felix faustusque dies."

CLAUDIAN.

EW, very few of Queen Victoria's present subjects remember her birth; and indeed it is only a minority of their number who can recall to mind her accession to the throne. Of the Judges and of the Bishops who witnessed that event not one survives; of the Houses of Peers and of Commons who formed the Parliament of her uncle at his decease, of his Privy Councillors, and of other public servants, few indeed remain to celebrate the Jubilee of her Majesty's accession; and their numbers diminish year by year.

In the course of time it has been Her Majesty's lot to outlive nearly every public servant of the Crown who held any high position when she came to the throne. The members of the Privy Council

52

of her predecessor ceased at his death to be Privy
Councillors; but, as a matter of fact they were all
re-sworn at her accession; and of those who wrote
themselves "Right Houourables" in June 1837,
only two survive, namely, Lord Ebury and Lord
Grey, then Lord Howick. Her Majesty has seen
the whole of the Episcopal and the whole of the
Judicial Bench renewed during her reign; and of
the members of the present House of Commons I
can recall only Mr. C. R. M. Talbot, Mr. Charles
Villiers and Mr. Gladstone, who were also members
of the last Parliament of William IV. The Peers
who held seats in one or other House of Parliament,
or at least their honours, in June, 1837, and who
still survive, are only the Marquis of Bath, Lords
Sydney, Ebury, Winmarleigh, Crewe, Nelson,
Granard, De Tabley, Portman, Lovelace, Eversley,
and Grey.

No more touching scene can well be imagined
than the moment of the Queen's accession to the
throne as a girl of eighteen. King William died
soon after midnight on the 20th of June, 1837, and
at five o'clock on that bright summer morning
the Princess Victoria was suddenly awakened in
her bed-chamber at Kensington Palace by the
Archbishop of Canterbury, and Lord Conyngham, who told her when she came down stairs
in her dressing-gown and slippers, and with
her long· hair flowing in disorder down her
back, that she was Queen of England. "She

burst," said the Archbishop, "into a flood of tears, and trembling and faint, as she thought of her new responsibilities fell down on her knees and entreated me to join with her in a prayer to heaven for grace to discharge the duties thus placed upon her."

The following longer and more detailed account of the affair I quote from the "Diary of a Lady of Quality:"—"At Kensington Palace the Princess Victoria received the intelligence of the death of William IV., in June, 1837. On the 20th, at 2 a.m., the scene closed, and in a very short time the Archbishop of Canterbury and Lord Conyngham, the Chamberlain, set out from Windsor Castle to announce the event to their young sovereign. They reached Kensington Palace about five; they knocked, they rang, they thumped for a considerable time before they could rouse the porter at the gate; they were again kept waiting in the courtyard; they turned into one of the lower rooms, where they seemed forgotten by everybody. They rang the bell, desired that the attendant of the Princess Victoria might be sent to inform H.R.H. that they requested an audience on business of importance. After another delay, and another ringing to inquire the cause, the attendant was summoned, who stated that the Princess was in such a sweet sleep she could not venture to disturb her. Then they said, 'We are come to the Queen on business of state, and even her sleep must give way to that,' It did; and, to prove that she did not keep them waiting, in a few minutes she came into the room in a loose white nightgown and shawl, her nightcap thrown off, and her hair falling upon her shoulders, her feet in slippers, tears in her eyes, but perfectly collected and dignified."

Lord Melbourne, the Premier, who, in spite of his constitutional indolence, arrived at the Palace by nine o'clock, at once had an interview with his new sovereign, and later in the day came the Lord Mayor, and Corporation of London to "worship the rising sun." I may quote a few words of Miss Martineau, to describe some of the incidents of that eventful morning : —

"On the meeting of the Princes, Peers, and other Councillors they signed the oath of allegiance; and the first name on the list was that of Ernest, King of Hanover. The Queen caused them all to be sworn in members of her Council, and then addressed them; after which they issued orders for the Proclamation of Her Majesty. If the millions who longed to know how the young Sovereign looked and felt could have heard her first address, it would have gone far to satisfy them. The address was, of course, prepared for her, but the manner and voice were her own, and they told much. Her manner was composed, modest, and dignified; her voice firm and sweet; her reading, as usual, beautiful. She took the necessary oaths, and received the eager homage of the thronging nobility without agitation or any awkwardness. The

declaration contained an affectionate reference to
the deceased King; an assertion of her attachment
to the constitution of the country, and of her intention to rule in accordance with it; a grateful
allusion to her mother's educational care of her;
an avowal that, under circumstances of such
eminent responsibility as hers, she relied for
support and guidance on Divine Providence; and a
pledge that her life should be devoted to the
happiness of her people. . . . . The first use
of the Great Seal, under the new reign, was to
authenticate the official proclamation, which was
gazetted the same evening. During the whole
morning carriages were driving up rapidly, bringing visitors eager to offer their homage. What a
day of whirl and fatigue for one in her position so
lonely, at such tender years! How welcome must
have been the night, and the quiet of her pillow,
whatever might be the thoughts that rested upon
it! The next morning she appeared ' extremely pale
and fatigued,' and no wonder, for she had passed
through a day which could never be paralleled."

The story of the Queen's accession, and of the
meeting of her first Privy Council, is thus told in
detail by Charles Greville in the first Series of his
amusing and gossiping "Memoirs":—"1837, June 21.
The King died at twenty minutes after two yesterday morning, and the young Queen met the Council
at Kensington Palace at eleven. Never was anything like the first impression she produced, or the

chorus of praise and admiration which is raised
about her manner and behaviour, and certainly not
without justice. It was very extraordinary, and far
beyond what was looked for. Her extreme youth
and inexperience, and the ignorance of the world
concerning her, naturally excites intense curiosity
to see how she would act on this trying occasion,
and there was a considerable assemblage at the
palace, notwithstanding the short notice that was
given. The first thing that was to be done was
to teach her her lesson, which, for this purpose,
Melbourne had himself to learn. I gave him the
Privy Council papers, and explained all that was to
be done, and he went and explained all this to her.
He asked her if she would enter the room accompanied by the great officers of state; but she said
she would come in alone. When the lords were
assembled, the Lord President informed them of
the King's death, and suggested, as they were so
numerous, that a few of them should repair to the
presence of the Queen, and inform her of the event,
and that their lordships were assembled in consequence; and, accordingly, the two royal dukes, the
two archbishops, the chancellor, and Melbourne,
went with him. The Queen received them in the
adjoining room alone. As soon as they had returned,
the proclamation was read, and the usual order
passed, when the doors were thrown open, and the
Queen entered, accompanied by her two uncles,
who advanced to meet her. She bowed to the

lords, took her seat, and then read her speech in a
clear, distinct, and audible voice, and without any
appearance of fear or embarrassment. She was
quite plainly dressed, and in mourning. After she
had read her speech, and taken and signed the oath
for the security of the Church of Scotland, the
Privy Councillors were sworn, the two royal Dukes
first by themselves; and as these two old men, her
uncles, knelt before her, swearing allegiance and
kissing her hand, I saw her blush up to the eyes,
as if she felt the contrast between their public and
natural relations; and this was the only sign of
emotion she evinced. Her manner to them was
very graceful and engaging. She kissed them both,
and moved towards the Duke of Sussex, who was
furthest from her seat, and too infirm to reach her.
She seemed rather bewildered at the multitude of
men who were sworn, and who came one after
another to kiss her hand; but she did not speak
to anybody, nor did she make the slightest difference in her manner, or show any in her countenance
to any individual of any rank, station, or party. I
particularly watched her when Melbourne and her
ministers, and when the Duke of Wellington and
Peel approached her. She went through the whole
ceremony, occasionally looking at Melbourne for
instructions when she had any doubt what to do,
and with perfect calmness and self-possession, but,
at the same time, with a modesty and propriety
particularly interesting and ingratiating. When
the business was done she retired as she had entered,

and I could see that no one was in the adjoining room."

The scene at Kensington Palace on the above occasion is thus described by Mr. Rush, from the lips of the late Lord Clarendon, one of the Privy Councillors present at the time:—" Lord Lansdowne, the president, announced to the Council that they had met on the occasion of the demise of the Crown ; then with some others of the body, including the Premier, he left the Council for a short time, when all returned with the Princess. She entered, leaning upon the arm of her uncle, the Duke of Sussex. The latter had not before been in the Council-room, but resides in the same palace, and had been with the Princess in an adjoining apartment. He conducted her to a chair at the head of the Council. A short time after she took her seat, she read the declaration which the Sovereign makes on coming to the throne, and took the oath to govern the realm according to law, and cause justice to be executed in mercy. The members of the Council then successively kneeled, one knee bending, and kissed the young Queen's hand as she extended it to each—for now she was the veritable Queen of England. Lord Clarendon described the whole ceremony as performed in a very appropriate and graceful manner by the young lady. Some timidity was discernible at first, as she came into the room in the presence of the Cabinet and Privy Councillors; but it soon disappeared, and a be-

coming self-possession took its place. He noticed
her discretion in not talking, except as the business
of the ceremonial made it proper, and confining
herself chiefly, when she spoke, to Lord Melbourne,
as official head of the Ministry, and to her uncle,
the Duke of Sussex."

The author of " The Diary of a Lady of Quality"
thus describes the first meeting of the Privy
Council of the youthful Queen, which differs only,
in some slight particulars from the accounts given
above : " The first act of the reign, was, of course,
the summoning of the Council, and most of the
summonses were not received till after the early
hour fixed for its meeting. The Queen was, upon
the opening of the doors, found sitting at the head
of the table. She received first the homage of the
Duke of Cumberland who, I suppose, was not King
of Hanover when he knelt to her. The Duke of
Sussex next rose to perform the same ceremony,
but the Queen, with admirable grace, stood up and
preventing him from kneeling, kissed him on the
forehead. The crowd was so great, and the arrangements were so ill made, that my brothers told me
the scene of swearing allegiance to their young
Sovereign was more like that of the 'bidding at an
auction' than anything else."

Sir John Hobhouse, who was present as a Privy
Councillor, draws a very slightly different picture
of the scene, he writes :—

" The Dukes of Cumberland and Sussex advanced

to receive her Majesty, and the young creature
walked in, and took her seat in the arm-chair. She
was very plainly dressed in mourning a black scarf
round her neck, without any cap or ornament on
her head ; but her hair was braided tastefully on '
the top of her head. She inclined herself gracefully on taking her seat. The Royal Dukes, the
Archbishops, the Lord Chancellor, and the Duke
of Wellington were on the right of her Majesty ;
Lords Lansdowne and Melbourne were on her left.
Soon after she was seated, Lord Melbourne stepped
forward, and presented her with a paper from which
she read her Declaration. She went through this
difficult task with the utmost grace and propriety;
neither too timid nor too assured. Her voice was
rather subdued, but not faltering, pronouncing all
the words clearly, and seeming to feel the sense
of what she spoke. Everyone appeared touched
by her manner, particularly the Duke of Wellington
and Lord Melbourne. I saw some tears in the eyes
of the latter. The only person who was rather
more curious than affected was Lord Lyndhurst,
who looked over her Majesty's right shoulder as
she was reading, as if to see that she read all that
was set down for her. After reading the Declaration her Majesty took the usual oath, which was
administered to her by Mr. Charles Greville, clerk
of the Council, who, by the way, let the Prayer
Book drop. The Queen then subscribed the oath,
and a duplicate of it for Scotland. She was

designated in the beginning of the oath 'Alexandrina
Victoria,' but she signed herself 'Victoria R.' Her
handwriting was good. Several of the Council,
Lord Lyndhurst, the Duke of Cumberland, and
the Duke of Wellington came to look at the
signature, as if to discover what her accomplish-
ments in that department were." At the close of
the long account from which this is a brief extract,
Mr. Hobhouse adds an extract written in his diary
on the day of the accession :—" it is impossible to
speak too highly of the Queen's demeanour and
conduct during the whole ceremony. They de-
serve all that has been said of them by all parties,
and must have been the offspring, not of art, nor
of education, but of a noble nature, to use the
wording of the well-turned eulogy pronounced
upon them by Sir Robert Peel."

Sir John Hobhouse was President of the Board
of Control, in other words, Secretary of State for
India, in Lord Melbourne's Ministry. As such he
had an audience of the Queen within a few days of
her accession. He shall tell his own story in his
own words :—

"I obeyed Her Majesty's commands, and went
to Buckingham Palace at the time appointed. The
apartments were in great disorder; housemaids
were on their knees scrubbing the floors, and
servants laying down the carpets. After waiting
a little time with a page, the door opened, and the
Queen walked in smiling and curtsying. She
placed herself on a sofa, on one side of a small

table, and desired me to take a chair opposite to
her. She told me that she had read Lord Elphinstone's letter, but had not had time to read Lord
Auckland's. She added that Lord Elphinstone's
was an interesting letter, and that he was very
young for so important a command. I smiled, and
observed that youth was no disqualification for
empire at all. Her Majesty laughed, and looked
pleased. She remarked upon the conduct of Sir
Peregrine Maitland, in refusing to allow the regimental bands to attend the Hindoo ceremonies.
She agreed with me in thinking it imprudent, and
that the zeal of some persons to propagate
Christianity, often defeated its own object. I
observed that Sir Peregrine Maitland was what was
called a 'serious' man. 'Yes,' replied Her Majesty,
'and his wife who is a sister of the Duke of Richmond, is serious also.' She told me she approved
of Lord Elphinstone's caution in that respect, and
desired me to tell him so; and she graciously
acceded to my request to convey her thanks, on
her accession to the Throne, to Lord Auckland for
his general conduct."

Not very long after this interview, Sir John
Hobhouse dined with the Queen at Windsor Castle.
After dinner, he writes : "The Queen sat down to
chess with the Queen of the Belgians. Her
Majesty had never played before ; Lord Melbourne
told her how to move, and Lord Palmerston also
assisted her. I looked on for some time without

taking part in the game, and I might as well have
abstained altogether, for when Melbourne and
Palmerston gave up advising Her Majesty, in order
that I might succeed to them, I did not succeed
better than my colleagues.   I was very near
winning the game when I lost it by an oversight,
and by being very often asked by Her Majesty,
'What must I do?'   There was also some little
confusion created by the two queens on the board,
and the two Queens at the table.   Her Majesty
was not so discouraged by her defeat as to prevent
her playing again the evening after this.   Who
played for the Queen I do not know; but her
Majesty ran up to me laughing, and saying she
had won.   She asked me how she came to lose
yesterday.   I replied, 'I suppose because your
Majesty had such bad advisers;' on which she
laughed heartily, and so did the Queen of the
Belgians, who, by the way, spoke English well."

"Sir David Wilkie," writes the author of "Old and
New London," "has painted the scene, but with a
difference.   The picture is well known to the public,
thanks to the engraver's art.   It may be a matter
of wonder that the Lord Mayor of London (Alderman Kelly) should have figured in this picture; but
the fact is that on the sovereign's death the Lord
Mayor is the only officer in the kingdom whose
commission still holds good; and, as such, he takes
his place, by virtue of his office, at the Privy
Council Board until the new sovereign is proclaimed."

The full text of Her Majesty's "Declaration" ran as follows:

"The severe and afflicting loss which the nation has sustained by the death of His Majesty, my beloved uncle, has devolved upon me the duty of administering the government of this empire. This awful responsibility is imposed upon me so suddenly, and at so early a period of my life, that I should feel myself utterly oppressed by the burden were I not sustained by the hope that Divine Providence, which has called me to this work, will give me strength for the performance of it, and that I shall find in the purity of my intentions, and in my zeal for the public welfare, that support and those resources which usually belong to a more mature age and to longer experience. I place my firm reliance upon the wisdom of Parliament, and upon the loyalty and affection of my people. I esteem also a peculiar advantage, that I succeed to a sovereign whose constant regard for the rights and liberties of his subjects, and whose desire to promote the amelioration of the laws and and institutions of the country have rendered his name the object of general attachment and veneration. Educated in England, under the tender and enlightened care of a most affectionate mother, I have learned from my infancy to respect and love the constitution of my native country. It will be my unceasing study to maintain the reformed religion as by law established, securing at the same time to all the full enjoyment

E

of religious liberty; and I shall steadily protect the rights, and promote to the utmost of my power, the happiness and welfare of all classes of my subjects."

It may be added for the gratification of those who are curious in such matters, that the original state paper, signed by the Queen — our present Magna Charta, is preserved and may be seen at the Public Record Office, in Fetter Lane, Fleet Street.

On the following day, June 21, the Queen was publicly proclaimed under the title of Victoria the First—the name Alexandrina, with which the first documents were prepared, being omitted by her when she first officially signed her name.[*]   At ten o'clock all the avenues to St. James's Palace were crowded; and as the guns fired a Royal salute the young Queen entered her palace amid the deafening cheers of her people.

"Garter" King-at-Arms was in the courtyard, with the Earl Marshal, the Duke of Norfolk, and attended by his heralds and pursuivants in their robes, and other officials; and, on the Queen's appearance at the window of the Presence Chamber, between Lord Melbourne and the Marquis of Lansdowne, he read aloud the proclamation of Victoria as "Queen of Great Britain and Ireland, Defender

---

[*] Mr. M'Gilchrist states in his "Public Life of Queen Victoria," that on the 21st of June the Queen was publicly proclaimed under the title of "Alexandrina Victoria," but that since that day she has disused the Russian name bestowed upon her by her Muscovite godfather, preferring to be styled simply "Victoria."

of the Faith." At its conclusion the Park and
Tower guns were fired, cheers rent the air, and the
Queen was for the moment overpowered, and
"throwing her arms on her mother's neck, she
wept without restraint." The Queen "looked exceedingly pale and fatigued, but her appearance was
interesting in the extreme;" and, notwithstanding
her evident grief of heart, she acknowledged with
grace and dignity the enthusiastic cheers with
which she was greeted by her new subjects. She
"was dressed in deep mourning, but with white
cuffs, tippet, and a border of white crape under a
small black bonnet, which was placed far back on
her head, showing her light hair simply parted over
her forehead."

The Queen remained in seclusion at Kensington
till after the funeral of the late King at Windsor,
on July 8; and on the 13th of the same month she
left the home of her childhood, with natural feelings of regret, and, accompanied by her mother,
went to reside at Buckingham Palace, where she
received addresses from the bishops, and members
of the two ancient Universities, and other public
bodies. "The Bishop of London told Amyot,"
. writes Crabb Robinson in his Diary in 1837, "that
when the bishops were first presented to the Queen
she received them with all possible dignity, and
then retired. She passed through a glass door, and,
forgetting its transparency, was seen to run off,
like a girl as she is. In corroboration of this, Mr.
Quayle told me that, lately asking a Maid of Honour

how she liked her situation, and who of course expressed her delight, she said, 'I do think myself it
is good fun playing at queen.' This is just as it
should be. If she had not now the high spirits of
a healthy girl of eighteen we should have less reason
to hope that she will turn out a sound, sensible
woman of thirty."

CHAPTER V.

THE QUEEN IN PUBLIC; HER MARRIAGE.

"Prodeas nova nupta."

CATULLUS, Epithal.

ARLY in June, 1837, the very last "Drawing Room" of the reign of William IV. was held at St. James's Palace; but owing to the illness of the King, which forced Queen Adelaide to remain by his bedside at Windsor, the Princess Augusta received the ladies in their stead.

The Queen's first Drawing Room, held in July, a month after she came to the throne, was looked forward to with the most intense interest in feminine circles. It is thus described by a venerable lady, only lately dead, who was present at it :—
"Necessarily, all were dressed in deepest mourning, our Sovereign herself wearing a black crape dress, embroidered in jet over black silk, train of crape, jet flowers, head-dress feathers, jet ornaments, and crape lappets ; her sombre toilette only relieved by

the Star of the Order of the Garter. This then,
was the first occasion when the English Court made
their obeisance to the Maiden Queen, and we remember how her royal bearing even then shone
conspicuous among all who surrounded her; that
young face and figure stands out in our memory, as
she receives the homage of her loyal subjects. The
following May the first birthday Drawing Room
was held, and then her Majesty appeared in a more
elaborate, and of course a coloured costume—a
white satin dress, with rich bullion fringe, the body
covered with splendid diamond stomacher, train of
white tabbinet, richly embroidered in gold, a handsome gold border to the train, which was lined with
white satin, and the materials were of English and
Irish manufacture."

The drawing room was crowded beyond all precedent, and the presentations of fair *débutantes*, as
might be expected, were very numerous, for all,
both young and old, were anxious to see the fair
flower of England, the maiden Queen, presiding
over her own Court, and doing its honours gracefully; and it is a natural instinct of women, as of
men, to " worship the rising sun " of royalty.

My lady readers may be glad to be informed
that when the Court mourning was at an end, the
young Queen wore a dress of English blonde over
white satin ; that the body and sleeves were ornamented with ribbon and blonde ; that she had a
train of handsome pink figured tabinet, tastefully

trimmed with ribbon and tulle, and lined with
white satin; and that her head-dress was adorned
with feathers and pearls.

For the following account, contrasting Drawing
Rooms of past days with those of the present, I am
indebted to a writer in the *Queen* newspaper:

"Long years of ceaseless change in dress and
custom have altered very materially the surroundings of these State Receptions. Our Queen was
present on this last occasion, in 1837; and we can
tell the exact costume worn by H.R.H. the Princess
Victoria. A special Court order had requested all
ladies to wear costumes of British manufacture,
which was generally obeyed—the Princess heading
the list in a dress of English blonde over white
satin; body and sleeves ornamented with ribbon
and blonde; train of handsome pink figured
tabbinet, tastefully trimmed with ribbon and tulle,
and lined with white satin; headdress, feathers and
pearls. All the dresses were simple as compared to
those of 1880. A skirt of very scanty width, just
touching the ground all round, perhaps with the
addition of a narrow flounce of lace or trimming,
was thought quite sufficient. A train and body of
another colour was most generally in fashion, and
this was but slightly trimmed. Perhaps a *bouquet
de corsage*, and one on each sleeve, might occasionally be added; but artificial flowers were not to be
seen as they are now.

"The headdress was very different from what has

of late years been admitted as court plumes. In
those days none could appear without white
feathers towering above the head, while another
drooped low on the shoulder, and was to be seen
on the left or right, accordingly as the wearer was
married or single. So high were the headdresses
when finally completed, that very few ladies could
sit in their carriages without removing the cushions,
and even then many stooped low to avoid collision
with the roof! Tulle veils were unheard of; rich
lace lappets had to be found and worn. A bouquet
in the hand was never carried. We are returning
to the gloves then worn, for they invariably reached
the elbow, and were generally trimmed with ribbon
and lace. As we recall these Drawing Rooms of
the past, we remember how many of the very
materials then in use are now so far out of date that
it would puzzle a *modiste* to recognise them. Trains
of tabbinet, skirts of areophane, and a material of
which whole dresses were often made (French
crape) can scarcely be got except in black. Passing
from changes in dress, let us recall the splendid
equipages which stand in single file up St. James's
Street, where they assembled by twelve o'clock, one
being the hour at which the Court began. A
brougham was then quite an unrecognised carriage,
and certainly for many years had no place in court
ceremonials. The family coach or chariot em-
blazoned with the arms, coachman in cocked hat
and wig, two tall footmen with canes standing
behind each carriage, were not the exceptions, but

the rule, and none ventured to appear save with some such state.

"The Birthday Drawing Rooms are no longer held. They were different from others, inasmuch as no presentations were then made, and it was etiquette for ladies to go on this day, even if they had been before in the season. No mourning could be worn, and the knights of the different orders all wore their collars. Until the death of the lamented Prince Consort, all the Drawing Rooms and Levees were held in St. James's Palace ; and, as Queen Victoria was the first sovereign who inhabited Buckingham Palace, which for some time was officially called the 'New Palace,' the days on which these courts were held afforded the people of London a frequent opportunity of seeing Her Majesty in some state, the procession from Buckingham Palace to St. James's under escort of troops bringing crowds into the park on each occasion. Tickets for a favoured few were also given for the hall at Buckingham Palace, to see the Queen pass to her carriage. Entering St. James's by the garden gates, and passing to the throne room. Her Majesty received any deputations whom custom admitted, as well as the captain of the Queen's Guard, who, going first into the Royal presence, received from Her Majesty's hand the parole for the day.

"The general company, on reaching the palace doors, set down in the long corridor, which was always lined with spectators admitted by ticket. Ascending the staircase, those who had the privilege of the *entrée* passed into one of the ante-chambers, and there waited till the doors opened, and they were ushered into the Throne Room. Passing through a double row of court officials, Ambassadors, and the Royal Household, it was some distance before the Royal presence was reached, when, duly passing on, they returned to the ante-room, and watch the less favoured crowd whose turn was now coming. In years gone by gentlemen might always attend the Drawing Room ; and sad indeed was the havoc made by spur and sword in the crush that was unavoidable under the old arrangements, and many were the rents and tears in lovely toilettes before the wearers reached Her Majesty's presence.

"During the reign of King William and his predecessors any lady on her presentation was kissed by the sovereign; in the same way a peeress, and the daughters of dukes, marquises and earls, now receive the same salutation from the Queen on their presentation. We have but little space to speak of the present, but the fashions and customs of this time can be seen by all; only a few can record their reminiscences of Queen Victoria as heiress to the throne, as maiden Queen, and youthful bride."

The young Queen's first musical *soirée* was most inconveniently crowded ; and she soon gave a state

concert, at which all the gentlemen remained standing. Within a short time of her accession she
presided over Chapters of the Orders of the Garter
and of the Bath, and everybody present, including
the officials of the Court and of the Heralds' College, was delighted at the grace and dignity with
which Her Majesty performed her part in those
ceremonies.

Early in the July of this year, before she had
been seated for a month upon the throne, the Queen
narrowly escaped injury from a carriage accident
on Highgate Hill. As she was descending the
steepest part of it in an open barouche, the pole
broke, and the horses were with difficulty stopped
from running away. The Queen and her party
took refuge, till the carriage could be repaired, in a
wayside inn, the "Fox," whose landlord was autho-
rised, in recognition of his services, to mount the
Royal Arms, and who to his dying day was very
proud of the honour of having entertained royalty
beneath his roof.

On the 17th of July, the young Queen went in
state to prorogue Parliament, in accordance with
constitutional usage on the demise of the crown;
and the people showed the greatest enthusiasm on
the route. Her Majesty "wore for the first time
on that occasion the garland-shaped diadem of
brilliants which is so peculiarly becoming to her,"
and she looked very animated and interesting, and
made a most favourable impression upon those who
were fortunate enough to see her.

On her arrival at the House of Lords the Queen
put on "her parliamentary robes of state of crimson velvet, entirely lined with ermine, and having
an ermine cape." Her Majesty ascended the
throne with a firm and composed step, for several
moments continued standing, graciously regarding
all around her. On the entrance of the Commons
the Speaker addressed the Queen, giving a brief
summary of the measures during the Session; and
then the Queen read her speech. In it she expressed her satisfaction at the mitigation of the
severity of the law with regard to capital punish-
ment. " I ascend the throne," she added, " with a
deep sense of the responsibility which is imposed
upon me ; but I am supported by the consciousness
of my own right intentions, and by my dependence
upon the protection of Almighty God. It will be
my care to strengthen our institutions, civil and
ecclesiastical, by discreet improvement, wherever
improvement is required, and to do all in my power
to allay animosity and discord. Acting upon these
principles, I shall upon all occasions look with confidence to the wisdom of Parliament and the affections of my people, which form the true support of
the dignity of the Crown, and ensure the stability
of the constitution." The graceful and dignified
manner in which Her Majesty delivered her speech
elicited from her uncle, the Duke of Sussex, a burst
of admiration," and he was heard to exclaim,
" Beautiful! beautiful !"; and all were struck with
her singularly clear and musical voice, which

without apparent effort, was heard distinctly in all parts of the House.

The Queen spent the first two months of her reign in town, and received numerous addresses of congratulation from various parts of the country. Towards the end of August the Court left for Windsor Castle, of which she then first took possession; and the whole line of route from London to Windsor was the scene of quite a triumphal procession, so many were the tokens of rejoicing and welcome. On the Sunday the Queen went to St. George's Chapel, and in the afternoon appeared on the Terrace with her mother and court.

"The immediate ceremonies of the Coronation," writes the author of the "Anecdotal Memoir of the Queen," "were followed by *fêtes* given by all the principal personages of the country, but more especially at Court, where the regal hospitality was extended on the most magnificent scale; not only to the British nobility, but to the illustrious foreigners who had collected in London to a greater extent than had been known since the visit of the allied Sovereigns of Russia and Prussia. Dinners, concerts, and balls succeeded each other rapidly at Buckingham Palace, the Queen herself forming the life and delight of the high-born assemblies. Her Majesty constantly danced twelve or fourteen quadrilles of an evening, and invariably closed the ball with a country dance. The fashion in which Her Majesty's partners are selected on these occasions

WINDSOR CASTLE.

has been thus described: The Lord Chamberlain, after the invitations have been issued, submits to the Queen a list of all those included in them who are eligible to the honour of Her Majesty's hand in the dance, and the Queen makes her own choice amongst them, herself marking the favoured few, in the order in which it is her pleasure to invite them ; when the Lord Chamberlain, previously to the opening of the ball, signifies to each of the noblemen so distinguished that Her Majesty does him the honour to command his attendance as her partner in the second, third, or fourth dance.

"It is refreshing to turn from this succession of gaieties," continues our author, "and to follow the Sovereign of this great empire into the stately and elegant retirement of Windsor, in which she was wont to indulge as soon as circumstances permitted after the celebration of this great national festival. But first let us take a retrospective view of a few weeks, to mark a beautiful instance of domestic and benevolent feeling. Mrs. Louis, the faithful and attached attendant of the late Princess Charlotte of Wales, in whose arms that lamented Princess expired, continued her residence at Claremont, high in the confidence of Prince Leopold, during the whole period of the young Queen's infancy and childhood. Delighted to contemplate in this youthful scion of royalty, not only a sterling resemblance in features and countenance to her beloved departed nursling, but the opening traits of a noble character in one destined to the same regal

career that formed the basis of so many hopes for
her, this venerable lady became enthusiastically
attached to the Princess, and did not fail to secure
for herself a grateful and affectionate return from
the innocent heart of childhood. Accordingly,
immediately after her accession to the throne, Her
Majesty invited Mrs. Louis to become a member of
her own family, though without any appointment
in the household, and furnished her with conve-
nient apartments in Buckingham Palace, conti-
guous to her own. Here she was in the spring of
1838, seized with her last illness, during which she
was watched over and consoled by the Queen of
England, with all the assiduous attention which
could have been bestowed by a young lady in the
middling classes upon a faithful and affectionate
nurse. Previous to the Easter holidays Her Majesty
left town for Windsor Castle, and her last act before
entering her carriage was to visit the death-bed of
her humble friend, with whom she spent a considerable time in such conversation as drew upon her
head the fervent blessings of the dying woman.
On quitting this distressing scene, Her Majesty,
feeling doubtless the improbability of her again
meeting the object of her present solicitude in this
world, threw herself into a chair in the adjoining
apartment, and burst into an agony of tears. When
somewhat recovered she repeated, with the earnest-
ness and frequency of real interest, her charge to
the attendants present, to watch over the comfort

of the invalid with the most scrupulous attention,
and thus, with a heart ill at ease, took her departure for Windsor.   No sooner had Her Majesty
alighted at the Castle than, throwing off her shawl
and bonnet, she proceeded to write with her own
hand to her beloved patient.   She told of her safe
arrival at the Castle, of the charming weather, and
exhilarating influence of the country breezes, and
closed her cheerful little note with renewed assur-
ances of affection and interest.   This, alas ! was
the last act of Christian charity that our amiable
Queen was permitted to perform to this valued
domestic, who expired two days afterwards, surrounded, by the care and bounty of her Sovereign,
with every auxiliary to her comfort and convenience.
A tablet has been placed in St. Martin's Church
by order of the Queen, commemorative of the
services of Mrs. Louis; and the kind friend who
tenderly nursed her through her fatal illness has
been presented by Her Majesty with a very valuable
gold watch, in testimony of her grateful recollection of her conduct on the melancholy occasion."

An anecdote of Her Majesty about this time is
worth repeating here.   The autumn months succeeding to the coronation season were passed by
Her Majesty at Windsor, in the usual interchange
of study, State-business, and out-of-door exercise,
particularly in her favourite recreation of riding;
and it was during one of these daily airings
that a curious incident occurred, reflecting equal

F

credit on both the parties concerned in the trans-
action. The equerry who was in immediate attendance on Her Majesty met in the long walk in
Windsor Great Park, his daughters also on horseback, and the Queen having kindly noticed them
en passant, signed to their father that he was at
liberty to converse with them ; he fell back accordingly, and the party remained for some few minutes
in earnest conversation.   On the return of the
equerry to the royal party the following dialogue
ensued : " Well, Colonel," said the Queen, " and
what had your daughters to say to you so earnestly
this morning ?"   " Some trifling remarks upon the
weather, and other such topics, please your Majesty."
" Aye, and what of me ?" rejoined the royal inter-
rogator.   " Your Majesty's good looks certainly
formed a part of our remarks," replied the Colonel.
" I confess," said the Queen, " that your daughter's
manner of looking at me attracted my attention,
and I am very desirous to know what she had
to say concerning me."   " And I," said her attendant, " must plead the privilege of family
intercourse, and entreat your Majesty not to press
me farther on the subject."   " Nay, but I insist
upon it," repeated Her Majesty, good humouredly,
but with the air of command.   " Then, madam,
your command shall be frankly obeyed, as I know
would best please you. My daughter, after remarking with pleasure upon your Majesty's healthful
countenance, and your apparent delight in horse-
manship, added, that it would render this agreeable

exercise more salutary, as well as wear a more graceful appearance, could you be induced to overcome the small stoop which is habitual to you, and to sit perfectly erect upon your horse." After a moment's consideration, Her Majesty smilingly replied, "I felt convinced that I had in some way or other fallen under the young lady's criticism, and was very anxious to profit by her observations; and now, my dear Colonel, I am equally obliged by your daughter's hint, and by your openness in repeating it at my desire, and will show you that I am not unmindful of either favour." "It was remarked with great pleasure by those about the Queen," continues the narrator of the above anecdote, " that she took pains from this time forward to sit very upright on her horse, which indeed was all that was wanting to render her an accomplished rider —possessing as she does all those attributes which so admirably qualify a lady to become a graceful and skilful horsewoman, moral qualifications as well as physical, for firmness and self-possession, or a power of controlling emotions, are as necessary to the perfect government of a horse, as elegance of shape and lightness of figure are essential to the graceful aspect of the person it bears. Her Majesty also evinces great taste in the style and character of the horse she selects for her use. Generally fourteen or fifteen hands high, her animal is always one of the very highest courage and breeding, well broken in, in the very best condition, of symme-

trical figure, aerial bearing, and of the gentlest
temper ; a gentlemanly horse in fact, one that is
conscious of the delicacy and rarity of its charge,
and who seems, as he paws the ground, to take a
pride in assisting to make her appear to the very best
advantage. Her Majesty, indeed, is at heart a horsewoman, and thinks that no lady looks to so much
advantage as when seated on her charger."

The visit to Windsor, which gave rise to the following characteristic description of Her Majesty,
was paid during the summer now on record, probably, by the reference to this habitual stoop, a
short time prior to the above-mentioned occurrence.
The writer observes : "On a recent visit to 'the
mighty Babylon,' my inclination led me thence
along the Great Western railroad to Windsor,
there to view the domain of ancient kings, and to
witness modern royalty in the novel form of one of
the beautiful daughters of Eve. I procured snug
quarters at the 'Star and Garter' on Saturday evening, and on Sunday morning repaired to St. George's
Chapel to hear Divine service. The service was
introduced by a voluntary from the organ, in the
midst of which our young Queen Victoria, accompanied by her mother, her uncle King Leopold
and his consort, the daughter of Louis Philippe, with
the other members of the Court, entered the royal
closet. The chapel was crowded, and many people
were compelled to stand throughout the whole
service of about two hours' duration. In the

afternoon I visited the royal gardens and terrace, where I found a goodly assemblage of people from various parts of the kingdom anxious to catch a glimpse of royalty. In a short time Queen Victoria appeared in the midst of her faithful subjects, accompanied by the Duchess of Kent, the King and Queen of Belgium, my Lord Melbourne, and a long list of noble lords and gentle dames, forming the court of the virgin monarch. They passed through the crowd to the slopes (a beautifully arranged plantation on the eastern side of Windsor Castle), and shortly afterwards returned, to the gratification of hundreds who had visited the place to see the Sovereign. As soon as the Royal party ascended the steps by the orangery into the gardens they passed the place at which I stood. Victoria hung on the arm of her uncle. The moment I saw her I observed to a friend, 'No painter has yet succeeded in giving to us a likeness of the Queen,' and such is really the case. She is low in stature, with a slight stoop in the shoulders, but womanly in appearance. With large, dark blue, expressive eyes, she has a fair and healthy countenance, and very agreeable, though not handsome, features. The face is more oval than is represented in any of the portraits, and her countenance is not childish as many of them would fain make us believe it to be. The ruddiness of her face appeared to us that of a young lady who had passed a month at the seaside, and paid much attention to her ablutions.

She was dressed with remarkable plainness, a light green silk shawl and white silk bonnet. She passed through the long line of living faces, evidently flattered by the curiosity excited by her appearance, and chatted pleasantly with her royal uncle. She subsequently walked on the eastern terrace, immediately under the royal apartments in view of the visitors to the gardens, but free from their interruption; it is about three hundred yards in length, and guarded at each end by a sentinel. On this beautiful promenade Her Majesty paced about for nearly an hour, her companions being first King Leopold, and next the Premier. The gay and sprightly manner in which the Queen walked seemed to put the pedestrian powers of Lord Melbourne to the test; with the aid of a stick he contrived to hobble along, but I fancied I saw in Her Majesty a sportive desire to play off a practical quiz on his lordship's disagreeable associate, the gout. Her style of walk is not the creeping, lifeless, ambulation that distinguishes many young ladies who affect to shine among the *haut ton*, she dashes off at a quick, buoyant pace, and maintains her movement with a peripatetic animation that would highly please my Lord Brougham, impelled onwards by a vigorous spirit, and something, as I imagined, like a hoydenish nature. Whenever the Queen arrived at either end of. the terrace, the sentinel presented arms, and the ladies and gentlemen of the Court formed opposite lines, through

which Her Majesty passed.   In this ceremony the
Queen appeared to me to assume an air of dignity
almost theatrical, which could not but force a smile
from the spectator.   In the midst of a jocund laugh,
she would suddenly compose her countenance to
the utmost gravity, compressing her pretty lips,
looking mysteriously towards the ground, and
injuring her sweet countenance by knitting her
brows.   The following day I had an opportunity of
seeing Her Majesty on horseback; she sat well on
her steed, but the stoop to which I have referred
was more perceptible in her riding habit than in
her more primitive dress.   She bowed gracefully
in acknowledgment of the homage offered to her
by the spectators, and seemed proud of the distinc-
tion to which she had arrived.   Her face shone
with good nature, and her eyes beamed with
affectionate respect towards all round.   She was
again accompanied by King Leopold, and his graceful Queen, who is a beautiful horsewoman, and wore
her beaver and feather with remarkable elegance."

Early in October the Queen left Windsor for
Brighton, where she spent a month ; along the road
she was received with acclamation, triumphal arches,
gay with festoons and flowers, were erected at several points on the journey, which was then of course
made by the high road ; and bouquets were presented at Croydon, at Reigate, and other places ;
and it was reckoned that a hundred and twenty
thousand persons were assembled to greet Her

Majesty at her entrance to the Pavilion. The return
to London was made in the same way.

On the 9th of November, the Queen went to the
City in state to be present at the Lord Mayor's banquet at Guildhall. The throng of people was
immense throughout the route, and her reception
enthusiastic. At Temple Bar, the Lord Mayor
(Alderman Pirie) and the city authorities received
Her Majesty according to ancient custom, deliver-
ing to her the keys of the city, which she handed
back into his safe keeping. The preparations made
at the Guildhall were of the most expensive description, and the gold service of plate used at the
dinner is said to have been valued at £400,000.
The Queen was accompanied by her favourite uncle,
the Duke of Sussex, the Duchess of Kent, and the
Duke of Wellington, most of her ministers and
officers of state, the judges, the bishops, &c. She
expressed to the Lord Mayor her great pleasure at
the entertainment. On her return to the palace in
the evening she was greeted again by enthusiastic
crowds, and a general illumination of the streets
and public offices took place; and a few days afterwards the *London Gazette* announced the bestowal
of a baronetcy on the Lord Mayor who had entertained her in such state. Our lady readers may
make, if they please, a note of the fact that on this
occasion Her Majesty was dressed in " pink satin,
shot with silver." It may also be recorded that
during this autumn she lived for a time at Marl-

borough House whilst Buckingham Palace was
under repair.

The Queen opened her new Parliament in state
by a speech from the throne in November, when
she confirmed the favourable impression which she
had created on the occasion of the prorogation in
July. Within the week she sent a message to her
faithful, loyal, and trusty Commons, expressing a
wish that a permanent provision should be made
for her mother; in consequence of which a bill was
passed, which settled upon the Duchess of Kent an
income of £30,000 per annum, while all parties
united in praise of the manner in which she had
superintended the education of her daughter. The
Queen's own civil list was settled during th same
session; it was fixed at £385,000 per annum, and
her privy purse at £60,000 more.

During the first few months of her reign the
newspapers gave an account, more or less authen-
tic, of the general routine of the Queen's daily life.
She generally rose early, often at six, and spent
some time in her own room in reading and writing.
At ten the Duchess of Kent came by invitation to
breakfast with her, and twelve was the hour for giving audiences to Cabinet Ministers. It may be noted
that the Queen always made herself acquainted
with the contents of all documents presented
to her before signing them. Her spare time she
devoted to reading or drawing; then there came
the afternoon drive or ride. After dinner, the Queen

frequently entertained her guests by singing popular airs, or there was a carpet dance, in which
she always took part ; being as fond of that pastime
as most young ladies of her age ; though not such a
devotée to "fandangoes" and "galliards" as was her
great predecessor on the throne, Queen Elizabeth.

The following year (1838) saw the splendid ceremonial of the Coronation, which, though shorn of
some of the festivities usual on such occasions, and
notably of the Champion's challenge and the banquet in Westminster Hall, was more gratifying to
the general public by a state procession through
the streets, which was substituted for them. The
day fixed was the 28th of June, and the sun shone
with more than usual brilliancy, as if to do honour
to the young Queen of that empire over which he
is said never to set.

Enormous crowds witnessed the outdoor pageant
as it slowly wended its way from Buckingham
Palace up Constitution Hill and along Piccadilly,
through St. James's Street, Pall Mall, and Charing
Cross, to the west doors of the venerable Abbey,
and it is reckoned that probably not less than
£200,000 were paid for the use of windows and
seats on the line of route. Special ambassadors
were sent over to represent their respective countries on the occasion; and the splendour of the
attire of some amongst them, especially Prince
Esterhazy, who was literally one blaze of jewels
from his head to his boots, formed a great attrac-

tion in the eyes of the multitude. In the early
morning all those who had the privilege of seats in
Westminster Abbey took possession of them, and
waited patiently till the arrival of the procession,
which made its way up the nave a little before
midday.

The great officers of State, the noblemen bearing
the regalia, and the bishops with the patina, chalice, and Bible received the Queen at the western
entrance. The list of the regalia, which are col-
lectively seen only on such occasions, comprised
"St. Edward's staff," carried by the Duke of Rox-
burghe; the "golden spurs," by Lord Byron,
(deputy to Baroness Grey de Ruthyn); the "sceptre
with the cross," by the Duke of Cleveland; the two
"swords of investiture" (of temporal and of spiritual
justice), by the Marquis of Westminster and the
Duke of Sutherland; the "curtana," or sword of
mercy, by the Duke of Devonshire; the "sword of
state," by Viscount Melbourne; the "sceptre with
the dove," by the Duke of Richmond; "the orb,"
by the Duke of Somerset; "St. Edward's crown,"
by the Duke of Hamilton; the "patina," by the
Bishop of Bangor; the "chalice," by the Bishop of
Lincoln; and the "Bible," by the Bishop of Win-
chester. The Duke of Norfolk, as Earl Marshal,
and the Duke of Wellington, as Lord High Con-
stable, stood on either side of Lord Melbourne.

The Queen, who bore her part in the long ceremonies of this day with perfect grace and dignity,

wore a Royal robe of crimson velvet, furred with
ermine and bordered with gold lace. She also wore
the collars of her Orders, and on her head a circlet
of gold. Her train was borne by eight daughters
of peers, namely (1) Lady Adelaide Paget ; (2) Lady
Caroline Amelia Gordon-Lennox ; (3) Lady Frances
Elizabeth Cowper ; (4) Lady Mary Alethea Beatrix
Talbot ; · (5) Lady Anne Wentworth-Fitzwilliam ;
(6) Lady Caroline Lucy Wilhelmina Stanhope ; (7)
Lady Mary Augusta Frederica Grimston ; and (8)
Lady Louisa Harriet Jenkinson. * Supported on
either side by the Bishops of Durham, and Bath and
Wells, the Queen advanced in procession towards
the altar, on which was placed a service of splendid
gold plate, and near to it St. Edward's chair. A
hearty welcome greeted her within the sacred
walls, and on the " recognition " of Her Majesty by
the Archbishop there was a general shout raised of
"God Save Queen Victoria !" The Queen made
her first offering of a pall, or altar cloth of gold,
and an ingot, or wedge of gold; the regalia were
laid on the altar. After the sermon which was

---

* Our readers may be interested in learning the fates of these ladies.
No. 1, married the Hon. Frederick William Cadogan ; No. 2, is Countess
of Bessborough ; No. 3, married Viscount Jocelyn, eldest son of the late
Earl of Roden, and died in 1880; No. 4, became by marriage Princess
Doria-Pamphili, and died at Rome in 1858 ; No. 5, married Sir John James
Randoll Mackenzie, Bart., of Scatwell, Ross-shire, and died in 1879 ; No.
6, married firstly Lord Dalmeny, and is now Duchess of Cleveland ; No.
7, became Countess of Radnor, and died in 1879 ; and No. 8, is the widow
of John Cotes, Esq., of Woodcote, Shropshire.

preached by the Bishop of London, Dr. Blomfield,
the Queen took the oath to defend the law and the
established religion, and she laid her right hand
upon the Gospel on the altar in confirmation of her
oath. Sitting in King Edward's chair, she next
gave her head and hands to be anointed by the
Archbishop. The regalia were delivered to her in
order, then the crown was taken from off the altar
by the Dean of Westminster, and handed to the
Archbishop, who placed it upon the Queen's head.
" God Save the Queen !" was shouted on all sides,
trumpets sounded, drums were beat, and the Tower
and Park guns were fired. Lastly, after the Bene-
diction and " Te Deum," the Queen was enthroned,
or " lifted " into the Chair of Homage, where she
delivered the regalia into the hands of the different
noblemen, and then received the homage of the
Princes and Peers, the Archbishop first kneeling to
do homage for himself and all his spiritual peers.
The Princes of the blood touched the crown, and
kissed the Queen's left cheek, and took the oath of
homage without kneeling. The peers knelt bare-
headed and kissed the Queen's hand. The venerable
Lord Rolle, " on advancing to pay his homage,
stumbled and fell back from the second step leading to the throne." He was raised up by two
noblemen, and reascended the steps, and, on presenting himself, the Queen " graciously advanced
to meet him, and, expressing her concern at the
accident, hoped he was not hurt." The Queen

afterwards received the Holy Communion, herself presenting the oblation of bread and wine, in accordance with ancient precedent.

On her return to the palace the immense crowds were gratified by the sight of the Queen wearing her crown, while the Princes and Peers and Peeresses all wore their coronets.

A brevet was issued by which a very large number of promotions were made in the army and navy in honour of the day; and several new Peers were created, and others advanced to a higher grade in the "roll of the House of Lords"; and this was accompanied by quite a shower of new Baronetcies. Already, indeed before she had sat for a month on the throne, she had raised to the Earldom of Leicester Mr. Coke of Holkham, and had bestowed a patent of Baronetcy on Alderman Wood, both old and staunch friends of her father and of her uncle the Duke of Sussex.

The Crown which had been made for George IV., weighed upwards of seven pounds; and, as it was considered too heavy for the Queen, a new crown of less than half the weight was constructed. It was formed of hoops of silver, covered with precious stones, over a cap of rich blue velvet, surmounted by a ball enriched with diamonds. Amongst its other gems was a large heart-shaped ruby which had been worn by the Black Prince; this was set in front of the circlet.

As the banquet in Westminster Hall was omitted

on the ground of economy, the interesting ceremony
of the " Champion and his challenge " formed no
part of the coronation festivities, and the Champion, Mr. Henry Dymoke, of Scrivelsby, Lincoln-
shire, was consoled for the omission by being
created a Baronet. The Queen entertained a hundred guests to dinner in the evening at Buckingham Palace, while State dinners were given by the
Cabinet Ministers. The theatres were open free, a
great fair was held in Hyde Park, and there were
general illuminations and fireworks. A grand review was held by the Queen in connection with the
rejoicings; a banquet was given at Guildhall, at
which Wellington, and the representative of France
at the Coronation, Marshal Soult, were included in
one and the same toast; and many special festivities
were held in various parts of the country, in honour
of the day.

Apart from the world of politics, with which we
have nothing to do, there is very little to record in
the period between the Coronation and the marriage of the Queen; the so-called " Bedchamber
Plot" forming the principal subject of interest; if
it was a plot, however, it was a very meagre one
indeed. The story of it runs as follows :—On Lord
Melbourne offering his resignation in April, 1839,
after obtaining the very small majority of five on a
question of importance with regard to the government of Jamaica, Sir Robert Peel attempted to
form a new administration; but as he was disap-

pointed in his supposition that the ladies who held
high office in the Household, and who were all
members of leading Whig families, would resign of
their own accord; and as the Queen, who had a
personal affection for the female members of her
Court, firmly opposed their removal, Sir Robert
Peel declined the task, and Lord Melbourne undertook office again. Though the Whig Ministers
were blamed for upholding the Queen in her opposition to Sir Robert Peel, the Queen herself
was rather admired by the people generally for her
natural and outspoken sincerity.

During the London season of 1839 the Queen
entertained the heir of the Russian throne, and
gave several balls and *fêtes* at Buckingham Palace;
and in the autumn King Leopold of Belgium and his
Queen paid a visit to her at Windsor Castle. But
yet 1839 was not an auspicious year. "The dubious
war in Canada—the unsettled state of the administration—the insurgent spirit at home—and, above
all, the injustice of party, which strove to make the
innocent young Queen accountable for the mistakes
made by some of her ladies in the case of the lamented Lady Flora Hastings—all combined to cast
a troublous shadow over the cold and wintry spring
of 1839." *

Of course at this time the nation thought a good
deal of the probability of the speedy betrothal of

---

* "Queen Victoria," Vol. II., p. 93.

the "Maiden" and the "Virgin" Queen, as she was
constantly styled in the newspapers; and the question was often asked on whom she would bestow
her hand in marriage. It was not very long before
all conjectures were set at rest. A Prince of the
House of Orange, Alexander of the Netherlands,
had been considered by William IV. to be the most
suitable choice for his niece; but, though her uncle
had other candidates in view as also eligible, the
Queen's wishes did not fall in with his, and she
wisely resolved to choose for herself, and to bide
her time.

It had so happened that Prince Albert, the second
son of Duke Ernest I., of Saxe-Coburg-Saalfeld,
and nephew of the Duchess of Kent, came to England with his father and brother in the summer of
1836, and stayed with his aunt at Kensington
Palace. The King and Queen Adelaide entertained
them at a *fête* at Windsor. The Prince was present with his Royal cousin, the Princess Victoria,
at the interesting annual gathering of the Charity
Children at St. Paul's, and they were afterwards
received by the Lord Mayor at the Mansion House.
No doubt the Prince was attracted by the fresh,
healthful beauty and charming grace of his cousin,
and the attachment seems to have been mutual.

The Prince made flattering mention of her in
many of his letters after this. He made the " grand
tour," visiting South Germany, Switzerland, and
Italy, in 1837-39; and early in the latter year, after

G

his return King Leopold spoke seriously to his
nephew, and wrote to his niece on the subject of
their possible union, and received a favourable
reply, though the Queen objected to any immediate
engagement. In the autumn of 1839 the Prince
again came over to England with his brother
Ernest, and pressed his suit in person. The Queen,
it is said, thought him much improved since his
former visit, and within a few days she told Lord
Melbourne that her mind was made up to the proposed union. It was commonly believed, or, at all
events, said, that the Queen signified her preference
for her cousin by giving him her bouquet at one of
the balls at the Palace, while the Prince, whose
uniform was " fastened up to the chin, seized a
penknife and slit an aperture in his dress next his
heart, and there triumphantly deposited the Royal
flowers." But this story, after all, may be apocry-
phal. It is said, too, that when the Prince expressed the great pleasure which he had experienced
from his visit to this country, the Queen asked him
if he would like to make it his home. The opportunity, we may be sure, was not lost on the Prince.

The Queen afterwards announced to him, at a
private interview, that she was willing to be betrothed to him, and, of course, there was no doubt
of the acceptance of the offer. Congratulations
poured in, and the Prince returned to Germany before bidding it adieu as his home. The appearance
of the Prince at this time is thus described by a

gentleman who was resident at Gotha : " Prince
Albert is a fine young man ; his complexion is clear,
his eyes of a greyish blue, exceedingly expressive,
his features are regular, the forehead expanding
nobly, and giving the notion of intellectual
power."

Mr. M'Gilchrist, in his " Public Life of Queen
Victoria," states it as an undoubted fact that this
marriage was " desired, if not planned, by certain
of their common relatives, especially the Duchess
Dowager of Coburg and her son, Prince (afterwards
King) Leopold, almost from the period when the
two cousins were in their cradles." He adds that
" after his betrothal the Prince himself told the
Queen that his mother, who died in 1831, had
earnestly desired their union."

The proposed marriage was announced by the
Queen herself to the Privy Council, and her " declaration " was published in the *Gazette*, and
received with pleasure by the nation. There were
difficulties as to the exact position which the Prince
should hold, and they were ended by the Queen
conferring on him a patent of precedence next
after herself.

On the meeting of Parliament in January, 1840,
the Prince's Naturalisation Bill and his Annuity
Bill were passed, the sum of £30,000 being agreed
upon—the Tories having successfully opposed the
original proposal by the ministry of £50,000. Mr.
T. Raikes states in his " Diary " that "the Queen at

first wanted £100,000, and that Lord Melbourne
had great difficulty in persuading her to consent to
the ministerial proposal of £50,000."

At the end of January, Prince Albert, his father,
brother and suite were escorted to England by Lord
Torrington * and Colonel Charles Grey, who had
already invested him with the insignia of the Order of
the Garter. The garter with which the Prince was
on this occasion invested was a present from the
Queen herself, and had been made with great care by
Messrs. Rundell and Bridge. The band was of
purple velvet, the motto of the order, the border,
and buckle were composed of diamonds, set in the
most exquisite taste; the whole, we are told, forming
an ornament in the highest degree brilliant and
unique.

The party crossed the Channel from Calais in
the "Firebrand," which was commanded by Lord
Clarence Paget; and, having received a hearty
welcome on landing at Dover and again at Canterbury, they arrived at Buckingham Palace on the
.8th of February. The Prince was welcomed at
the entrance by the Queen and her mother; and

---

* Lord Torrington was to the very last, a personal favourite of the Queen,
by whose desire he always held a post in the household, whether his own
party (the Whigs) were in office or not. He died in 1884. Colonel Grey,
afterwards better known as General Grey, was for many years prior to his
death in 1870, Private Secretary to H.R.H. the Prince Consort, and was
afterwards confidentially employed by the Queen. He edited her "Journal
of Our Life in the Highlands."

the same afternoon he took the oaths of allegiance
and supremacy, which were administered to him by
the Lord Chancellor, Lord Cottenham. The commission which gave him the rank of a Field
Marshal in the army bore the same date.

Unlike many royal marriages, the union of the
Queen with Prince Albert was from the first
extremely popular with the nation at large; and
the reason was not far to seek: it was because it
was understood to be "based," as Lord Melbourne
said, "not upon reasons of state policy, but upon
personal choice and predilection."

On the 10th the marriage was celebrated at the
Chapel Royal, St. James's. It is almost needless to
say that an immense crowd was collected in the
park to view the *cortège* between Buckingham Palace
and St. James's. The bridegroom's procession
went first to St. James's, and the Prince was accompanied by his father and brother. He wore a field-
marshal's uniform, the breasts of his coat being
decorated with bride's favours. The Queen was
escorted by her mother and the Duchess of Sutherland, and, we are told, "she looked pale and
anxious." The scene in the courtyard of the palace
was gay enough for summer owing to the numerous
shades of colour of the ladies' dresses and the
various uniforms of the officials in attendance.

The Archbishops of Canterbury and York, and
the Bishop of London officiated at the ceremony.

The altar was laden with gold plate of the value, it is said, of £10,000. The Duke of Sussex gave away the bride, who wore a rich " white satin dress with a very deep trimming of Honiton lace ; the body and sleeves were richly trimmed with the same material to correspond; the train was of white satin, and was also lined with white satin, and trimmed with orange blossoms. On her head the Queen wore a wreath of orange blossoms and a veil of Honiton lace, with a necklace and earrings of diamonds. The cost of the lace alone on the Queen's dress was £1,000. The satin, which was of a pure white, was manufactured in Spitalfields. Her Majesty wore an armlet, inscribed with the motto of the Order of the Garter, ' *Honi soit qui mal y pense*'; and she also wore the Star of the Order."

The Queen was attended at the altar by twelve bridesmaids, unmarried daughters of some of the noblest families of the kingdom, several of whom two years before had officiated as train bearers at her Coronation. They were as follows:—(1) The Lady Adelaide Paget; (2) The Lady Sarah F. C. Villiers; (3) The Lady Frances Elizabeth Cowper; (4) The Lady Elizabeth West; (5) The Lady Mary Augustus F. Grimston; (6) The Lady Eleanor C. Paget; (7) The Lady Caroline A. G. Lennox; (8) The Lady Elizabeth A. G. Howard; (9) The Lady Adelaide Hay; (10) The Lady Catherine Lucy Wilhelmina Stanhope; (11) The Lady Harriet

Pleydell Bouverie; (12) The Lady Mary Charlotte Howard.*

The Wedding Breakfast was given at Buckingham Palace; the cake (we are told) weighed 300lb., and was three yards in circumference, and four-teen inches in depth. " It was described by an eye-witness as consisting of all the most exquisite compounds of all the rich things with which the most expensive cakes can be composed, mingled and mixed together with delightful harmony by the most elaborate science of the confectioner. On the top was a device of Britannia blessing the bride and bridegroom, who were dressed somewhat incon-gruously in the costume of ancient Rome. At the foot of the bridegroom was the figure of a dog, intended to denote fidelity; at the feet of the Queen was a pair of turtle doves. A host of gamboling Cupids, one of them registering the marriage in a book, and bouquets of white flowers tied with true lovers' knots, completed the decora-

---

* It may interest our readers to learn what has become of these twelve ladies during the half century which has since passed by. No. 1, is now the Hon. Mrs. Frederick W. Cadogan ; No. 2, died in 1853, having married Prince Nicholas Esterhazy ; No. 3, afterwards Viscountess Jocelyn, and mother of the Earl of Roden, died in 1880 ; No. 4, is Duchess of Bedford ; No. 5, was Countess of Radnor, and died in 1879 ; No. 6, married the late Sir Sandford Graham, and died young ; No. 7, is now Countess of Bess-borough ; No. 8, is now the wife of the Hon. and Rev. F. R. Grey ; No. 9, died several years since, the wife of the Earl of Gainsborough ; No. 10, is now Duchess of Cleveland ; No. 11, married in 1847 William Ellice, Esq. ; No. 12, is now the Dowager Lady Foley.

tions."* At the conclusion of the repast the Royal
pair set off for Windsor Castle, where they spent
four days. Our lady readers may be interested in
learning that Her Majesty's travelling dress was
"a white satin pelisse, trimmed with swansdown,
and a white satin bonnet and feather." On their
return to Buckingham Palace the chief amusements
of the Queen and her Consort consisted of levées,
"dinners followed by little dances" and visits to
the theatres. The Queen's next birthday was
spent at Claremont, a place to which she was much
attached,† and which she frequently visited; both
she and her husband were glad to escape there
from time to time, from the smoke and oppressive-
ness of town, and, perhaps, also from the equally
oppressive grandeur of Windsor Castle.

The Queen paid another visit to Brighton, not
long after her marriage; but on this occasion the
royal pair were so much annoyed by the eager and
rude curiosity of many inhabitants and visitors,
that they did not return to the Pavilion, which
indeed, Her Majesty never again visited, and
resolved, from that time, to dispose of; but, being
very fond of the sea, and wishing to have a quiet
marine residence, Her Majesty purchased Osborne
House, near Cowes, in the Isle of Wight, from
Lady Isabella Blachford. The old house, a moderate

* " Public Life of Queen Victoria," by John M'Gilchrist.

† See pages 47 and 48.

sized and comfortable mansion of the eighteenth century, was pulled down, and the present edifice, in the Italian style, was erected in its stead, from the designs of the Prince Consort, carried out by the late Mr. Thomas Cubitt. Her Majesty and the Prince constantly added to the estate as land came into the market, and the property now amounts to about 2,000 acres, so laid out that Her Majesty can drive for eight miles without quitting her estate.

Osborne has always been a favourite resort of the Queen, and of late years she has generally spent both Christmas and Easter there, as well as some weeks in the summer. It may be interesting to our readers to learn that about half-a-mile from the house is a "Swiss Cottage," with kitchen, dairy, &c., where the young princesses, in former days, amused themselves by making themselves practically acquainted with domestic economy; and a museum containing objects of natural history, collected by the royal children in the course of their tours at home and abroad. Close to the cottage are the gardens formerly cultivated by their own hands, and from which it is said that the Princess Imperial of Germany still has vegetables regularly forwarded to her in her Prussian home.

In the early summer of the year of her marriage the Queen experienced one of those attacks from which few of the crowned heads of Europe would seem to be exempt; for, as she was driving with the Prince up Constitution Hill, a youth named

OSBORNE.

Oxford fired two pistol shots at her. Happily no injury was caused, and the Queen showed the utmost courage and presence of mind on the occasion. Her first thought was to let her mother see that she was unhurt, for fear of the news being, as is usually the case, exaggerated. Oxford was supposed to be insane, but was tried for the offence, and was ordered to be confined during Her Majesty's pleasure. The Queen has been the object of other attacks of a like kind on several occasions since this: In May, 1842, close to the same spot, John Francis fired a pistol at Her Majesty. It was not certain whether it was loaded with ball. The man was sentenced to undergo the extreme penalty of the law for high treason, but by the Queen's clemency, the sentence was commuted to one of transportation for life. In July of the same year a deformed youth named Bean presented a pistol loaded with powder and wadding alone at the Queen as she was driving to the Chapel Royal. In May, 1850, an ex-lieutenant of Hussars, Robert Pate, struck the Queen with a small switch and cut her face, as she was driving out of Cambridge House; and in February, 1872, a youth, by name O'Connor, presented a pistol and a Fenian document at Her Majesty as she was entering Buckingham Palace on her return from her public visit to St. Paul's. In March, 1882, another young man named Roderick Maclean fired, or pretended to fire, at the Queen in the yard of the Railway Station at Windsor. The offenders

were all sentenced to various punishments—none
perhaps so severe as they deserved.

The Queen has been more frequently annoyed
by (happily harmless) insults of another kind than
is probably generally known or remembered.
Several madmen have followed her at times with
the intention of declaring their love for her; and a
certain Captain Goode was for some time notorious
for persistently following her about in his
brougham. But we are anticipating the order of
events.

The great interest of the latter part of the year
1840 was the birth of the Princess Royal, now
Imperial Princess of Germany. The event happened on the 21st of November, a little before the
time expected, but the Queen's health did not
suffer. The christening of the infant Princess took
place in the Throne Room of Buckingham Palace on
Feb. 10th, 1841, the first anniversary of the Queen's
Wedding. The sponsors were the Dowager Queen
Adelaide, the Duchesses of Kent and Gloucester,
the King of the Belgians, and the Dukes of Sussex,
and of Saxe-Coburg and Gotha. She received the
names of Victoria Adelaide Mary Louisa. In December, 1840, the superintendence of the Royal Nursery
was entrusted to the charge of Mrs. Kempthorne,
the widow of a former rector of St. Michael's,
Gloucester.

Mr. Raikes writes as follows in his amusing
"Journal":—"All who went to the Prince of

Wales's christening say that the scene was very magnificent, and the display of plate at the banquet superb. After the ceremony a silver embossed vessel, containing a whole hogshead of mulled claret, was introduced, and served in bucketfulls to the company, who drank the young Prince's health. Very few ladies were invited."

The following year, 1841, was, in many ways, the least auspicious of all during the Queen's reign. The condition of the people had been declining, and there was in consequence a bad spirit abroad in many parts, and the register of crimes of violence, especially in connection with what was known as Chartism, became a very dark one. It was this state of things which hastened the establishment of free trade a few years later But, on the 9th of November, the birth of the Prince of Wales at Buckingham Palace, gave a brightness to its close. Complaints, however, were heard on account of the feasting, which was held at Windsor, while there was so much distress in the country during the long winter months, and for some time after this, the Royal Family lived in comparative quiet.

The infant Prince was born Duke of Cornwall, and on the 4th of December, following, it was announced in the *Gazette*, that Her Majesty had been graciously pleased to issue a patent creating her infant son, Prince of Wales and Earl of Chester, &c., &c., in conformity with the established practice. He was christened at St. George's Chapel, Windsor, on January 25th, 1842, and received the names Albert Edward, after his illustrious father and grandfather. The sponsors were, the King of Prussia, Prince Ferdinand of Saxe-Coburg, the Princess Sophia, and the Duchesses of Saxe-Coburg and Saxe-Gotha. The name of the Prince, for nearly half-a-century, has been so identified with that of the Queen, his mother, and more especially since her widowhood, that we can hardly think of them apart; and, he has lived so much in public, that happily, we are not called at present, to write his biography.

> "And for the mother's sake we loved the boy!
> And dearer seemed the mother for the child."

It may be well here to anticipate the order of events, and give a list of Her Majesty's other children, two of whom are already grandmothers, viz. :— The Princess Royal, mentioned above; Princess Alice, who became the wife of H.R.H. The Grand Duke of Hesse; Prince Alfred, Duke of Edinburgh, who is married to the Princess Mary of Russia; Princess Helena, the wife of Prince Christian of Schleswig-Holstein; Princess Louise, Marchioness of Lorne; Prince Arthur, who is married to the Princess Margaret of Prussia; Prince Leopold, who married Princess Helena of Waldeck, and died just two years afterwards; and lastly, Princess Beatrice, wife of Prince Henry of Battenberg.

CHAPTER VI.

HER HOME TOURS AND TRAVELS.

"Instar veris enim vultus ubi tuus
Affulsit, populo gratior it dies.
Et soles melius nitent."

HORACE.

OWN to the present reign few of our Hanoverian Sovereigns had seen much of their own dominions; but one of the characteristics of our Queen has been her love of making tours, and of visiting the principal places of interest in her kingdom. We have seen that in her childhood she was a great traveller. It was not, however, very easy for her to gratify this taste after her accession, whilst she was unmarried; but after the birth of her two first children scarcely a summer passed by in which she did not make a journey by land, or voyage by sea to some part or other of her dominions. In this portion of our biography we have as a guide her Majesty's own published "Journal."

It was not until the second year of her married

111

life that the Queen commenced those visits, or
"progresses"—to use the word so familiar to the
readers of the reign of Queen Elizabeth,—which she
afterwards made from summer to summer to the
houses of the most distinguished of her subjects.
These visits, however, happily, did not involve the
stiff and costly ceremonial which the "progresses"
of Elizabeth entailed on those of her subjects who
entertained her; but though the immense extravagance of the *fêtes* given in the olden time at
Kenilworth was not repeated at Belvoir or at
Chatsworth, or any other lordly seats, on the
occasion of the visits of Victoria, her welcome, we
may rest assured, has not in the latter cases been
less cordial or sincere.   Woburn Abbey, the home
of the Russells, was the first house so honoured by
her Majesty after her accession.   The royal *cortége*
travelled by road across from Windsor to Woburn
on Monday, the 2nd of August, 1841, the "progress"
of the Queen and the Prince causing a general
rejoicing in all the towns and villages through
which they passed.   From Woburn, on Thursday,
the 5th, they went on to Panshanger, near Hertford,
the seat of Earl Cowper; and on the following day
they visited the Premier, Lord Melbourne, at
Brocket Hall, in the same neighbourhood, receiving
an address from the loyal town of Hertford and
from the inhabitants of the county.   On the next
day, Saturday, they returned back to Windsor by
road.

In this year (1841), political events changed.
The Whigs who had held office under Lord
Melbourne as Premier, gave way to the Conservative Party headed by Sir Robert Peel. With the
exception of this event nothing of importance
occurred till the autumn; but the strong personal
attachment of Her Majesty to Lord Melbourne,
who had been so to speak her preceptor, made it
rather difficult for her to treat Sir Robert Peel with
equal confidence and regard.

It was in the early autumn of 1842, when the
Queen first set eyes on that Scotland, in which she
was afterwards destined to find her home. At the
end of August, the royal yacht, attended by eight
"satellites," sailed, or rather, steamed away from
Woolwich. The Queen was accompanied by Lord
Liverpool, Lord Morton, General Wemyss, Colonel
Bouverie, Mr. G. E. Anson, Sir James Clark, the
Duchess of Norfolk, and Miss Matilda Paget. On
September 1st, they landed at Leith, visited
Edinburgh, staying at Holyrood Palace, and
Dalkeith (where the Queen held a Drawing Room),
and then went on by land to Perth and .Dunkeld,
being the guests successively of the Duke of
Buccleuch, Lord Mansfield, the Duke of Athole,
the Marquis of Breadalbane, and Lord Willoughby
de Eresby. On their return journey, they visited
Rosslyn and several other places of interest, and left
Edinburgh on the 15th of September, after spending
a most enjoyable fortnight north of the Tweed.

Early in September, 1844, took place the christening of Prince Alfred, who was so named in com-
pliment to our Saxon King Alfred. Immediately
after this, the royal party again made a yacht
voyage to Scotland, and spent a fortnight in
Perthshire and Aberdeenshire, with Blair Athole as
their head-quarters. It was at this time, probably,
that the Queen first thought seriously of making
Scotland a home for a portion of each year, as its
beauties and the homely manners of its people
had, by this time, much attracted her. " Lord
Aberdeen," observes the Queen, " was much
touched, when I told him that I was so attached to
the dear, dear Highlands, and missed the fine hills
of Scotland so much. There is," adds the Queen,
" a great peculiarity about the Highlands and
Highlanders; they are such a chivalrous, fine
active people. Our stay among them was so
delightful. Independently of the beautiful scenery,
there was a quiet, a retirement, a wildness, a
liberty, and a solitude, that had such a charm for
us." . . . . " We were very, very sorry to
leave Blair and the dear Highlands. Every little
trifle, and every spot I had become attached to ;
our life of quiet and liberty, everything was so
pleasant, and all the Highlanders and people who
went with us, I had got to like so much. Oh! the
dear hills, it made me very sad to leave them
behind."

The next few years of our Queen's life, were

uneventful, and interrupted only by the birth of
Princess Helena.

As soon as Parliament was prorogued, in August,
1847, the Queen and Prince again made a yacht
voyage from Osborne to Scotland, this time sailing
up its western coasts, touching *en route* at Dart-
mouth, Truro, Penzance, the Scilly Isles, Milford
Haven, the Menai Straits, and the Isle of Man.
At every place, the greatest enthusiasm was shown.
At Truro, the youthful Prince of Wales, who is
also Duke of Cornwall, was held up in his father's
arms, to be introduced to the Cornishmen and
Cornishwomen, over whom, he is one day, destined
to reign.

On the occasion of this tour, they made the
acquaintance of the Western Highlands, and visited
Inverary Castle, the residence of the Duke of Argyll.
Here occurred an incident related in Her Majesty's
" Journal," which is now of more than common
interest, since one of the children mentioned by
the Queen is now her son-in-law. " The pipers
walked before the carriage, and the Highlanders on
either side, as we approached the house. Outside,
stood the Marquis of Lorne, just two years old, a
dear, white, fat little fellow, with reddish hair, but
very delicate features, like both his father and
mother; he is such a merry independent little child.
He had on a black velvet dress and jacket, with a
' sporran,' scarf, and Highland bonnet." From
Inverary the royal party journeyed by land, and

reached their Aberdeenshire quarters early in September.

It is from this visit that the Queen's idea of purchasing Balmoral must be dated: at all events, we have from Her Majesty's own pen, an account of the Royal Family's first stay in the Castle during the following autumn, when it was rented by the Queen, and from which time it has become a favourite home to her.

The old Castle at Balmoral was a fine and handsome structure, quite in a castellated style; a view of it is given on page 59 of " Leaves from Our Journal in the Highlands." Our readers will be glad to read in connection with it Her Majesty's " First impressions " of the place. She writes under date Friday, September 8th, 1848: " We arrived at Balmoral at a quarter to three. It is a pretty little castle, in the old Scottish style. There is a picturesque tower and garden in front, with a high wooded hill; at the back there is a wood down to the Dee, and the hills rise all around. There is a nice little hall, with a billiard-room; next to it is the dining-room. Ascending by a good broad stair-case upstairs, immediately to the right and above the dining-room is our sitting-room, formerly the library, a fine large room; next to this is our bed-room, opening into a little dressing-room, which is Albert's. Opposite, down a few steps, are the children's and Miss Hildyard's three rooms. The ladies live below, and the gentlemen upstairs."

The royal pair were not long in making acquaintance with the place; for on the day of their arrival,
as soon as lunch was over, they ascended the wooded
hill, to get a view of the house and the River Dee.
The Queen describes the prospect, in her "Journal,"
in a few short lines, and adds with a touch of simple
nature, "it was so calm and so solitary, it did one
good as one gazed around, and the pure mountain
air was most refreshing. All seemed to breathe
freedom and peace, and to make one forget the
world and its sad turmoils." In all probability, not
many days had passed by before the Queen and the
Prince Consort had resolved that, if Balmoral could
be bought, they would become the purchasers.

In her "Leaves from Our Journal in the
Highlands," the Queen herself tells us how it
came to pass that she and the Prince Consort
became the owners of the estate of Balmoral,
which, in the olden time, was part of the broad
lands of the Gordons of Huntly, of the Erskines,
Earls of Mar, and of the Farquharsons, before it
passed into the hands of the Earl of Fife, by pur-
chase in 1799. "In 1830," writes Her Majesty,
"Sir Robert Gordon, brother of Lord Aberdeen,
obtained from Lord Fife's trustees his first lease of
Balmoral; but the terms of the lease not being
considered satisfactory, a second lease for a term of
thirty-eight years was subsequently obtained This
second lease was purchased by the Prince Consort
from Lord Aberdeen in 1848, after Sir Robert

BALMORAL.

Gordon's death, and the fee simple of the estate was finally purchased from the Fife trustees in 1852. The first additions made to Balmoral by Sir R. Gordon were commenced in 1834, the kitchen, offices and square tower in 1835, other additions were made in 1836, the wooden tower or turret was added in 1838, and the whole building was completed in the following year. The deer park had been made as far back as 1833."

Balmoral, as it now stands, was built adjoining the old castle, between 1853 and 1855; it is a fine building, in the castellated style, and quite in keeping with the neighbourhood and the mountain scenery. Its plan and arrangements are due to the skilled hand of the late Prince Consort, who took a deep interest in the work in all its details, and in the laying out of the grounds. It is on this account that this place has always had such a special attraction for Her Majesty, as she herself tells us repeatedly.

Her Majesty, under date September 7th, 1855, describes the arrival of herself and the Prince at their new home in the Highlands. "At a quarter-past seven, we arrived at dear Balmoral. Strange, very strange, it seemed to me, to drive past, and indeed, *through* the old house; the connecting part between it and the offices being broken through. The new house looks beautiful. The tower and the rooms in the connecting part are, however, only half finished, and the offices are still unbuilt;

therefore, the gentlemen (except the Minister of
State in attendance) live in the old house, and so
do most of the servants; there is a long wooden
passage which connects the new house with the
offices. An old shoe was thrown after us, into the
house, for good luck, when we entered the hall.
The house is charming; the rooms delightful; the
furniture, the papers, in fact, everything perfection."
Her Majesty gives us two coloured engravings of
the interior of her own and of the Prince's rooms,
which certainly wear an air, not of state, but of
comfort and repose; and she tells us, that the
slight alteration of the site chosen for the new
house, enables her from her windows to command
a view of the valley of the Dee, with the mountains
beyond, which could not be seen from the old
house.

The "good luck" solicited for the new house,
by the throwing of the old shoe above-mentioned,
was not long in coming; for, on the 10th of the
same month (September, 1855), arrived a telegram
from Sir James Simpson announcing that Sebastopol was in the hands of the allies. The same
evening, the good news was spread all round the
country, by a huge bonfire lighted on the top of a
"cairn" on the hill-side by the Prince and gentlemen of the Court.

In the autumn of this year it was publicly announced that the Princess Royal was betrothed to
Prince Frederick William of Prussia. Her Majesty

thus records the event in her "Journal," under date September 29, 1855: "Our dear Victoria was this day engaged to Prince Frederick William of Prussia, who had been on a visit to us since the 14th. He had already spoken to us on the 20th, of his wishes; but we were uncertain, on account of her extreme youth, whether he should speak to her himself (now) or wait till he came back again. However, we felt it was better that he should do so; and during our ride up Craig-na-Ban this afternoon, he picked a piece of white heather (the emblem of 'good luck'), which he gave to her; and this enabled him to make an allusion to his hopes and wishes, as they rode down Glen Girnoch, which led to this happy conclusion."

The Princess Royal had laid so firm a hold upon the affections of the nation, although she had not been brought prominently before it, that it was with deep reverence, the people on the occasion of her marriage indicated their esteem by presenting addresses of congratulation to our Queen and her Royal Consort as well as to the young bride so soon transplanted to a foreign land.

Her Majesty's love for Balmoral is a subject on which she never tires of descanting in her "Journal." Thus she writes in October, 1856: "Every year my heart becomes more fixed in this dear paradise, and so much more so now that all has become my dear Albert's own creation, own work, own building, own laying out, as at Osborne;

and his great taste and the impress of his dear hand
have been stamped (upon it) everywhere. He was
very busy to-day settling and arranging many
things for next year." We may be sure that her
love for and attraction to, the place have been
increased by the circumstances under which she
has of late years visited it.

Year after year, at first during the late summer
and autumn, but now, for several years past, in the
late spring as well as in the autumn, has Her
Majesty retired to her Highland home; and the
Court Circular has told us week by week, when
her health has permitted, of her long drives and
excursions in the bracing mountain air, and of her
friendly visits to her neighbours and her tenants.
Many, too, have been her kindly acts to the sick
and poor of that wild district, which, quite apart
from Her Majesty's "Journal," have reached the
ears of not a few of her subjects.

A simple but touching extract from the "Journal,"
describing a Sunday at Craithie, may find a fitting
place here:

"Went to Kirk as usual; service by the Rev.
Norman Macleod. The sermon extempore, simple,
and yet so eloquent. Text from the coming of
Nicodemus to Christ by night, (John iii.) The
preacher showed how all tried to please self, and
live for that, and in so doing found no rest. Christ
had come not only to die for us, but to show us
how we ought to live. The second prayer very

touching.   His allusions to us were so simple,
saying, after his mention of us, ' Bless their
children.'   It gave me ' a lump in my throat.' "

Truly has it been written that "one touch of
nature makes the whole world kin.", "A lump in
the throat" is an affection to which we are all
more or less liable, from the Queen to the peasant.
Medical men may shake their heads and ascribe it
to hysteria; but the affection is one of the heart ·
rather than the throat.

Towards the end of the summer of 1868, under
the name of the Countess of Kent, Her Majesty saw
the Alps for the first time.   She spent a few weeks
at Lucerne, when she ascended Monte Pilato and
other mountain peaks, riding her Highland pony.
She occupied the Villa, Wallis, and lived in quiet
simplicity, free from state and ceremony.   During
her stay there she visited the shores of Lago
Maggiore, and saw most of the other beautiful
scenes in that lovely borderland of Italy and
Switzerland.

In the same year Her Majesty allowed her name
to be enrolled among the "Royal and Noble
Authors of England," by publishing "Leaves from
the Journal of our Life in the Highlands," a work
remarkable for its simplicity and for the genuine
appreciation alike of fine scenery and of the
domestic element of life which it displays.   In this
book Her Majesty has taken her subjects quite into
her confidence, drawing up the curtain from much
of her private life, and giving expression to her

personal tastes and opinions with much freedom and good sense.

The book was edited by the late Sir Arthur Helps, and published in a handsome quarto volume with several exquisite steel and wood engravings, and with a few specimens of Her Majesty's own sketches of stags brought down by the Prince's rifle in deer-stalking, or "bits" of scenery as seen from the deck of the Royal yacht. It is dedicated to the Prince in the following brief but touching terms:—" To the dear memory of him who made the life of the writer bright and happy, these simple records are lovingly and gratefully inscribed." The book was afterwards reprinted, without the illustrations, in a smaller and cheaper form.

The book, as Sir Arthur Helps tells us in his editorial preface, was designed by its author at first to be "printed privately for presentation to members of the Royal Family and Her Majesty's intimate friends, especially to those who had accompanied and attended her in her tours;" but he adds that afterwards, a fear arising lest some portion of its contents, or incorrect representations of its contents, might find their way into the public journals, "it was thought better to place the volume within reach of Her Majesty's subjects."

"Moreover," adds the editor, "it would be very gratifying to her subjects, who had always shown a sincere and ready sympathy with the personal joys and sorrows of their sovereign, to be allowed to

know how her rare moments of leisure were passed
in her home, when every joy was heightened, and
every care and sorrow diminished by the loving
companionship of the Prince Consort, with whose
memory the scenes to which this volume refers
would always be associated.

The Queen has shown in all the positions she
has occupied, and not least as a kind and good
mistress of her household, and her attachment to
many of her attendants is well known ; in some
cases members of succeeding generations of the
same family have been attached to her service.
Many of these "old friends" she mentions with
affection in her "Journal," and in some cases gives
interesting records of their services in detail.
Among these is one whose name is probably
familar enough to our readers—Mr. John Brown,
the especial attendant of Her Majesty in most of
her Highland excursions, and whose merits as a
royal servant are thus recorded with a sketch of
his biography by the Queen herself.

"The same who in 1858 became my regular
attendant out of doors, everywhere in the Highlands, who commenced as gillie in 1849, and was
selected by Albert and me to go with my carriage.
In 1851 he entered our service permanently, and
began in that year leading my pony, and advanced
step by step, by his good conduct and intelligence.
His attention, care, and faithfulness cannot be
exceeded, and the state of my health which of late
years has been sorely tried and weakened, renders

such qualifications most valuable, and indeed most needful, in a constant attendant upon all occasions. He has since (in December, 1859), most deservedly been promoted to be an upper servant, and my permanent personal attendant. He has all the independence and elevated feelings peculiar to the Highland race, and is singularly straightforward, simple-minded, kind-hearted, and disinterested, always ready to oblige, and of a discretion rarely to be met with. He is now (1868) in his fortieth year; his father was a small farmer who lived at the Bush on the opposite side to Balmoral. He is the second brother, three of whom are in Australia and New Zealand, two are living in the neighbourhood of Balmoral, and the youngest, Archie (Archibald), valet to our son Leopold, is an excellent trustworthy young man."

In November, 1880, Her Majesty lost the services of her faithful attendant, who died suddenly, at Windsor, from the effects of a chill, caught in executing a commission of his royal mistress.

We can give only a brief notice of some of the principal occasions in which the Queen has appeared in public, and of the most notable of her journeys or excursions, other than those to which we have already specially alluded. Her Majesty has lived in comparative retirement, during the later years of her reign, and most of the principal events and scenes, in which she has taken part, and which go to make up the history of this period, are fresh in the recollection of many of our readers.

In August, 1843, after a yachting excursion around the Isle of Wight, and about the South Coast, the Queen and Prince Albert extended their trip to Treport, on the French coast, and went thence to pay a visit to Louis Philippe, at his country residence, the Chateau d'Eau, where their reception was of a most costly description. This visit did not raise the French Citizen King in the Queen's estimate. Three years afterwards Mr. Raikes writes in his "Journal," that " The Queen is very much incensed against Louis Philippe. She says, that he has not only been guilty of a low dishonest political intrigue, but he has forfeited his word of honour, as a gentleman, to *her personally*, while pretending the most sincere friendship. She would not allow his picture to be put up in the castle, and would not be disinclined to go to war with him." Early in the following summer, the Emperor Nicholas of Russia, paid a visit to the Queen, and was magnificently fêted at Windsor.

In the August of 1845, the natural attractions of the land which was the early home of the Queen's mother and her husband, must have made their visit there a most enjoyable one. The Queen and Prince embarked at Woolwich in the "Fairy" steamer, and passed up the Rhine to Cologne and Mayence, whence they visited Coburg and the Castle of Rosenau, the Prince's birthplace, where they occupied the room in which the Prince was born.

Cambridge was honoured by a visit from the

Queen on the occasion of the installation of Prince
Albert as Chancellor of the University, in July,
1847, when the poet Wordsworth's "Installation
Ode," was performed; and it is needless to add, that
the undergraduates were conspicuous for their loyal
and hearty welcome of their Sovereign.

Disturbances were rife in Ireland in 1848; but in
the following year one of the fruits of the restora-
tion of peace in the land was a visit of the Queen
to the Emerald Isle. She was accompanied by
Prince Albert and their two eldest children, and
was escorted by a squadron to the Cove of Cork,
which in consequence received the name of Queens-
town. Her reception, both in Cork and Dublin,
was most enthusiastic, and there is no doubt that
the visit was well-timed, and had an influence for
good on the nation. In the August of 1858, the
Queen and Prince Consort visited Germany, where
they were received by the King and Queen of
Holland and other distinguished personages. During
their stay in Germany the royal pair honoured Berlin
with a visit, and a meeting took place between the
Princess Frederick William and her Royal mother.
A Berlin letter says: "The meeting between the
Queen of England and the Princess Frederick
William, her daughter, was very affecting. The
Princess sprang into the carriage to her Royal
mother, and the two remained clasped in each
other's arms for some time, unable to speak."

CHAPTER VII.

MARRIED HAPPINESS.

"Felices ter it amplius"
                HORACE, Od.

HE opening of the Great Exhibition in Hyde Park, the parent of so many International Exhibitions in this and other countries, will ever be associated with the history of the year 1851. It was formally opened by Her Majesty in person, and with much ceremonial. The initiative of this fairy-like palace, and its success, were due to the forethought and guidance of Prince Albert; and, though the long "era of peace" which it was expected to inaugurate did not follow on it, there can be no question but that it had an immense influence in promoting the social and artistic welfare of the nations of the world. It was visited by an immense number of persons from all parts of the country, as well as by thousands of foreigners. From its ashes, so to say, arose the Crystal Palace

at Sydenham, which also, opened by the Queen
herself, in June, 1854, has been the means of afford-
ing instruction and amusement to some millions of
visitors from all parts of the world.

Among the International Exhibitions to which
the original one of 1851 gave rise, were those of
Dublin in 1853, which was honoured by a visit
from the Queen during the summer of that year,
and in 1855 the first in Paris, in the building which
still stands in the Champs Elysées. The Queen
crossed the Channel to see it, and was the guest of
the Emperor at St. Cloud, where, as well as in
Paris, great fêtes were held in her honour. The
Emperor and Empress of the French had been
entertained by the Queen at Windsor Castle in the
April of this year ; and during their stay they
witnessed a review of the *élite* of Her Majesty's
troops in Windsor Park, and they were everywhere
received with cordiality. They also visited the
City, and the Queen invested the Emperor with
the Order of the Garter, and gave a State banquet
in his honour in St. George's Hall.

On the opening of this great Exhibition, the
Queen writes :—" The great event has taken place
—a complete and beautiful triumph—a glorious and
touching sight, one which I shall ever be proud of,
you, my beloved Albert, and my country. . . .
Yes, it is a day which makes my heart swell with
pride and glory, and thankfulness ! We began it
with tenderest greetings for the birthday of dear
little Arthur. At breakfast there was nothing but

congratulations. . . . Mamma and Victor were
there, and all the children and our guests. Our
humble gifts of toys were added to by the beautiful
little bronze *replica* of the Amazon (Kiss's) from
the Prince (of Prussia), a beautiful paper-knife from
the Princess (of Prussia) and a nice little clock from
mamma. The park presented a wonderful spectacle,
crowds streaming through it, carriages and troops
passing, quite like the Coronation Day, and for me
the same anxiety—no greater, on account of my
beloved Albert. The day was bright, and all bustle
and excitement. . . . At half-past eleven the
whole procession in state carriages was in motion.
. . . . The Green Park and Hyde Park were
one densely crowded mass of human beings, in the
highest good humour and enthusiasm. A little
rain fell as we started, but before we came near the
Crystal Palace the sun shone out and gleamed upon
the gigantic edifice, upon which the flags of all the
nations were floating. We drove up Rotten Row
and got out at the entrance on that side. The
glimpse of the transept through the iron gates, the
waving palms, flowers, statues, myriads of people
filling the galleries and seats around, with the
flourish of trumpets as we entered, gave us a sensa-
tion which I can never forget. We went for a
moment to a little room where we left our shawls,
and where we found mamma and Mary (now Princess
of Teck), and outside which were standing the
other Princes. In a few seconds we proceeded,
Albert leading me, having Vicky at his hand, and

Bertie holding mine. The sight, as we came to the middle, where the steps and chair (on which I did *not* sit) were placed, with the beautiful crystal fountain just in front of it, was magical,—so vast, so glorious, so touching. One felt—as so many did to whom I have since spoken—filled with devotion, more so than by any service I have ever heard. The tremendous cheers, the joy expressed in every face, the immensity of the building, the mixture of palms, flowers, trees, statues, fountains, the organ (with two hundred instruments and six hundred voices, which sounded like nothing), and my beloved husband, the author of this 'Peace Festival,' which united the industry of all the nations of the earth,—all this was moving indeed, and it was and is a day to live for ever. God bless my dearest Albert! God bless my dearest country! which has shown itself so great to-day. One felt so grateful to the Great God! Who seemed to pervade all and to bless all! The only event it in the slightest degree reminded me of was the Coronation; but this day's festival was a thousand times superior. In fact, it is unique, and can bear no comparison, from its peculiarity, beauty, and combination of such different and striking objects. I mean the slight resemblance only to its solemnity; the enthusiasm and cheering, too, were much more touching, for in a church generally all is silent."

A few weeks after the opening of the Great Exhibition, Her Majesty dined in state with the Lord Mayor at the Guildhall, to receive with due honour the Commissioners of the Exhibition and the representatives of foreign nations. It was observed at the time, that in 1839 she had entered the city in state to inaugurate a new Temple of Commerce (the Royal Exchange), and that in 1851 she went through the same ceremony to celebrate the inauguration of a novel Palace of Trade.

In October of the year 1854, on their way back from the north to London, the Queen and the Prince Consort visited Hull and Grimsby in the steamer " Fairy," and at the latter place opened the new docks which are the chief attraction of that ancient town.

The Crimean War, which proved to be but the beginning of an era of disturbance in Europe, broke out in the spring of the same year, and was the great subject of interest alike to the Queen and her people. The names of Alma, Inkerman, and Sebastopol will not be unworthy to rank with older names on many of the regimental colours of England's army. But the glory was not won without severe loss and suffering from wounds and lingering sickness and disease in the hospitals, brought on by the terrible privations and long night watches in the trenches during the severe winter. The Queen, on whom their sufferings and bravery made a deep impression, visited many of her wounded soldiers, who were brought home during the war, in the hospital at Chatham; and in May, 1855, she publicly presented medals on the parade of the Horse Guards to many of the invalided officers and non-commissioned

officers and men of her army. On handing the
medal to Sir Thomas Troubridge, who had lost
both his feet at Inkerman, she at the same time
gracefully made him one of her aide-de-camps.
"Upon every occasion during the continuance of
the war," writes Mr. J. M'Gilchrist, "the Queen
showed the most heartfelt sympathy with her brave
soldiers ; visited their hospitals and transport ships ;
received the wounded at her palace ; and suggested
and liberally assisted in the establishment of permanent means of relief for them and their families.
A beautiful letter of the Queen, which was accidentally made public about this time, showed that in the
privacy of domestic life the Queen did not forget
these sufferers. Indeed, she complained that she was
not kept sufficiently informed of the needs of those
who had returned to their country wounded in its
service." She was also most constant in her visits
to her wounded soldiers at Fort Pitt, Chatham, and
the other military hospitals.

The Queen also afforded great encouragement to
the Volunteer movement, which was revived and
carried on with great spirit in 1859, and which the
late war had helped to encourage. Early in the
following summer the Queen showed her hearty
interest in the movement by holding a special levee
for the presentation of volunteer officers at Court.
She also graced the first Wimbledon Meeting of
1860 with her presence, fired the first shot and
established an annual prize of the value of £250.
During the same season she held a review of over

twenty thousand volunteers in Hyde Park, and
another review of the Scottish Volunteers at
Edinburgh.

In the autumn of 1861 the Queen once more
honoured Ireland with a visit; this time she accepted the hospitality of Lord Castlerosse and
Mr. Herbert of Muckross at their seats amid the
exquisite scenery of the far-famed Killarney lakes.
the native beauties of which she explored and
admired.

This year, 1861, will be long remembered as that
which brought at its close the severest trials which
the Queen has undergone. The Duchess of Kent,
who had been so good a mother and the guide of
her childhood, died early in the year; but that loss
was one which could not but have been looked for
sooner or later, for the Duchess had reached the
allotted span of human life. It was destined, however, to be cast into the shade by another and far
heavier bereavement. During the autumn the
Queen and Prince had stayed as usual with their
family at their Scottish home, and soon after their
return the Prince visited his son the Prince of
Wales, who was studying at Cambridge. He appeared for the last time in public with the Queen
at a review of the Eton College Volunteer Rifle
Corps in the Castle grounds at Windsor, when he
caught a feverish chill, and, though no alarm was
felt at first for what was thought might be only a
passing malady, typhoid fever set in, and the Prince
breathed his last on the evening of Saturday,

December 14, deeply mourned by the Royal Family
and indeed by the whole nation.

> "Sweet nature, gilded by the gracious gleam
> Of letters, dear to science, dear to art,
> Dear to thy land and ours, a Prince indeed,
> Beyond all titles, and a household name,
> Hereafter, through all time—Albert the Good."

The Prince Consort's body was laid at first in
the royal vault at St. George's, Windsor; but Her
Majesty built at Frogmore, on the confines of
Windsor Park, a splendid mausoleum for its reception, to which it was afterwards removed. The
Queen, and the members of the family who are
with her, regularly visit the tomb on the anniversary of the Prince's death and funeral. In honour
of the late Prince Consort the Queen has most
richly embellished the Wolsey Chapel at Windsor,
and has in consequence re-named it the "Albert
Chapel."

The inscription in Latin, on the Prince's coffin
may be translated as follows:

> Here lies the most exalted and illustrious Albert, Prince
> Consort, Duke of Saxony, Prince of Saxe Coburg and Gotha.
> Knight of the most noble Order of the Garter, the most beloved
> husband of Queen Victoria, who died on the 14th December,
> 1861, in the 43rd year of his age.

The Latin was from Dean Stanley's pen, but the
substance was dictated by the Queen herself.

No words can be more fitly applied to the late
Prince Consort than those of the poet:

> "—For that he loved our Queen,
> And, for her sake, the people of her love.
> Few and far distant names shall rank above
> His own, where England's cherish'd names are seen."

It is almost needless to add the Queen felt her great loss most deeply; but still she bore up at the time courageously, and her great desire thenceforth was to be able to fulfil her duty towards her children and the nation, though bereft of the light of him whom Tennyson, addressing the widowed queen, so truly styles:

> " That star
> Which shone so close beside thee that ye made
> One light together, but has past, and leaves
> The crown a lonely splendour."

So prolonged was her Majesty's grief, and her consequent seclusion, that in the year 1866-67 it became the subject of comment in the public newspapers, and for a time just a cloud of unpopularity overshadowed her. *The Saturday Review* especially remarked in terms of bitter irony on her conduct; and even suggested that it might be well for her to entrust a part of her royal duties to her eldest son. But the cloud soon passed away, and gradually Her Majesty braced up her nerves for the discharge of her duties, though her appearances in public were very " few and far between."

It is much to be regretted Her Majesty did not for many years appear at the head of her Court in London, a Court which in her married life she had done so much to purify by her presence and her example— the influence of which, in the interests of morality, it is impossible to over-estimate.

H.M. THE QUEEN.

CHAPTER VIII.

THE QUEEN AS A WIDOW.

"Sola domo mœret vacuâ."
VIRGIL, Æn. iv.

THERE is no doubt that Her Majesty's nervous system was terribly shaken by her sorrow; and in 1871 the nation became more than usually anxious about her.

In that year Dr. Norman Macleod spoke as follows at Glasgow, with reference to the health of the Queen :—

"I have had the honour, in the providence of God, of ministering to her Majesty in public and private for the last thirteen or fourteen years. I have seen her in every variety of circumstances, from the highest prosperity and happiness which any married woman, not to speak of a Queen, could enjoy, and also in the depth of her distress. I declare most solemnly I have never in the greatest privacy, and in the most intimate communion, that

a subject or a clergyman can have, heard one word
offered, or one sentiment expressed, which did not
do the highest honour to her Majesty, both as a
queen and as a woman; I have never seen, not even
the remotest trace, of any moral or mental weak-
ness, but I have seen in every instance, down to
the last moment, remarkable evidence of moral and
mental strength and capacity. I am very glad to
say that from the severe attack of neuralgia and
rheumatic gout (which so affected the Queen's
hands that for a time she was unable to sign her
name) she has entirely recovered. I have never
seen her in better spirits and stronger in mind than
she is at present. At the same time, I am far from
saying that she has recovered her strength so as to
be able to do more than she is doing; indeed I am
certain that the Queen has done all that her nervous
energy permits her to do. Our own wives find
how trying to the nervous energy are the constant
cares of a large family; but when we think what
the Queen has to do as a mother, with her children
occupying such important positions in society—
what she had to do in being compelled often to
think about the affairs of the nation, to whose
interest she is profoundly devoted; when we think
of the constant weight that must ever be upon her
mind—the wonder is that she is able to perform
her duties as she has done. Anyone who knows
the Queen knows that she would do all that it is
possible for her to do; and no one who knows her
is amazed at her extraordinary considerateness for

everyone—how she occupies her thoughts upon every subject, and how she attends to such minute detail of her duty, that I will take it upon me to say that the care of the poorest subject in her kingdom, if made known to her, would receive her immediate attention. Let me also say that it is a cruel and cowardly injustice the manner in which her Majesty is often criticised, when she cannot make any reply, but must endure in silence. But, while these criticisms are made by the few, I feel certain that the huge majority of this nation so revere the monarch who occupies the throne, and so admire her unblemished personal character, and the manner in which during her reign she has discharged her public and private duties, that could they utter it one voice would unite with ours when we say, ' God save the Queen.' "

It appears that the heated atmosphere engendered in crowded assemblies acts on the Queen exactly as sea-sickness does with most of us; it creates nausea which nothing but going to bed will relieve ; and her personal discomfort is certainly not diminished by the necessity which also exists in these ceremonials of standing for hours on her feet.

In spite of her seclusion, Mr. D'Israeli in 1871 bore willing testimony to Her Majesty's habits of strict attention to all public business that claimed her attention, though "physically incompetent for the discharge of mere ceremonial duties."

But happily there have been some joys to light up the clouds and relieve her great sorrow. The

Prince of Wales was married, with the good wishes of the nation, in March, 1863, at St. George's, Windsor, to Alexandra, the lovely and beloved Princess of Denmark; and the constant presence of the Heir Apparent and his charming wife, during the London season, at Marlborough House has in some degree made amends for the absence of the Sovereign from Buckingham Palace and the Court of St. James's.

The Queen went late in the summer of 1868, with Prince Leopold and the Princesses Louise and Beatrice, to Lucerne, where she resided for a time under the title of "Countess of Kent." Here she enjoyed numerous excursions through the neighbourhood, and gained benefit to her health. She left England once again for Germany, to visit the grave of her half-sister, who died in September, 1872.

The Queen has been always ready to forward any works of utility or of charity, and when able, has graced their inauguration with her presence. For instance, in November, 1869, she was seen in public in the City, where she went to open the new bridge at Blackfriars and the Holborn Viaduct. She also laid the first stone of the new St. Thomas's Hospital, which now, removed from Southwark, faces the Houses of Parliament on the Surrey side of the Thames; and in 1876 she went to the East End to open the new wing of the London Hospital.

Towards the end of the autumn of 1871 the Queen passed many anxious days on account of the severe illness of the Prince of Wales at Sandringham, and she herself went to his bedside. The nation shared in the anxiety, and there came a feeling of great relief when his gradual recovery set in about the middle of December. It was a memorable day, that 27th of February, 1872, when the Queen accompanied her son through a dense crowd of her people to St. Paul's Cathedral, to offer thanksgiving to God for his recovery. The scene in the cathedral was most striking, and the reception of the Queen and her son almost overwhelming, so great was the enthusiasm of the nation.

The Queen herself published in the *Gazette* a letter addressed in the person of Mr. Gladstone to the nation, to express the depth of her feelings and gratitude on the occasion. We shall be excused for reprinting it. The text of it ran as follows:—

Buckingham Palace,

February, 29th, 1872.

The Queen is anxious, as on a previous occasion, to express publicly Her *own* personal *very deep* sense of the reception She and Her dear Children met with on Tuesday, February 27th, from Millions of Her Subjects, on Her way to and from St. Paul's.

Words are too weak for the Queen to say how very deeply touched and gratified She has been by the immense enthusiasm and affection exhibited towards Her dear Son and Herself, from the highest down to the lowest, on the long progress through the Capital, and She would earnestly wish to convey her warmest and most heartfelt thanks to the whole Nation for this great demonstration of loyalty.

The Queen as well as Her Son and dear Daughter-in-law, felt that the whole nation joined with them in thanking God for sparing the beloved Prince of Wales' life.

The remembrance of this day, and of the remarkable order maintained throughout, will for ever be affectionately remembered by the Queen and Her Family.

On this memorable day the Queen gave £1,000 and the Prince of Wales £500 to the "Special Thanksgiving Fund," which was opened for the completion of St. Paul's Cathedral; and both Her Majesty and her son inscribed their names in a new subscription book.

1874. This summer the nation learned with as much pleasure as surprise that the Queen had so far awoke from her long "retreat" as to dance at a Highland ball at Balmoral.

"We can imagine," says one of the weekly papers, "the delight with which a Pepys of the nineteenth century would enter in his Diary the fact that the Queen has at last danced. From old chroniclers we hear that Queen Elizabeth delighted her grave Lord Keeper, Sir Christopher Hatton, by dancing a fandango; but history has been notoriously unjust to that beautiful, learned, and witty princess, in persisting to remember her only as 'good Queen Bess,' and 'old Queen Bess,' and to forget the long years during which she was not only young, but the most beautiful queen in all Europe. The daughter of Harry Tudor and Anne Boleyn must, by Mr. Darwin's law of natural selection, have been beautiful even in her old age; and why we should clothe Mary of Scotland with beauty, with her powders, patches, paints and her

thirty various wigs of divers colours, and laugh
because Elizabeth of England jumps up to show
Sir Christopher how a figure should be executed, is
one of the puzzles of history. Loyal subjects will
not therefore laugh when they hear that after
thirteen years of melancholy widowhood, her
Majesty, says the *Pictorial World*, has opened the
ball at Balmoral Castle not with a grave Lord
Keeper, but with one who has been advanced to be
an esquire in attendance—one of her gillies, whose
name is well known for his faithful adherence.
That which is done in the north may as well be
done in the south ; and perhaps after a rehearsal at
Windsor in the great hall, and amongst her loyal
nobles, we may hope to see smoke ascending from
the chimneys of Buckingham Palace, and hear of a
succession of balls in that hitherto deserted and
dreary building. The ubiquitous eye of the press,
never absent from a court gathering, has watched
over Balmoral, and the fact that the Queen has
danced is now known over Europe. It does not
matter, now the magic observance is broken, how
soon it is broken again; and if courts and palaces
are any use at all, the sooner the Queen dances
amongst her loyal courtiers—as well as amidst her
gillies, servants and tenants—the better."

In the summer of 1875 occurred an unfortunate
episode in the Queen's life, and one which occasioned
her intense grief. On its passage from Osborne to
Gosport, the royal yacht, which conveyed Her
Majesty and some other members of the royal

family, under the command of Prince Leiningen.
unhappily ran into one of the yachts which were
just then crossing the path of the Queen and cut it
down, the sad consequence being the loss of two
lives, including that of a member of the family of
her owner. In' consequence of this misadventure,
since that time the royal yacht has gone at a slower
rate of speed in crossing the Solent.

The Queen in 1874 saw her second son, Alfred,
Duke of Edinburgh, married to the only daughter
of the Emperor of Russia, and has witnessed the
marriage of all her daughters; the last to leave her
being the Princess Beatrice, who remained as the
constant companion of her widowed mother. The
Queen's grandchildren are numerous—twenty-five
are recorded in the Peerage as now living—and the
eldest daughter of the Princess Imperial of Germany,
who was married in 1878 to the Duke of Saxe-
Meiningen, is the mother of a young family.

Her Majesty has of late years appeared again
from time to time among her people on important
occasions when her health has permitted. She
opened the session of the New Parliament in 1866,
and also the two Sessions of Parliament in 1876
and 1877, in person, though she did not on these
occasions assume her state robes, and deputed the
Lord Chancellor to read her speech to the assembled
Houses.

In September, 1876, the Queen had a narrow
escape from a serious accident. Her Majesty was
taking a long drive from Balmoral to Kildrummy

Castle, a distance of forty miles. While proceeding through Ballater, one of the horses in the royal carriage fell. The others were with some difficulty reined in, and the fallen horse, springing to its feet, was trying to dash off at great speed, when a policeman courageously ran up to it, seized the bridle, and succeeded in stopping it. Fortunately, no one was injured. Her Majesty remained quite cool, but much alarm was felt by the attendants.

It is but lately that another title has been added to those which the Queen already possessed, that of " Empress of India," a title which was publicly proclaimed to the assembled princes and people of India at Delhi on the first day of the year 1877. The Bill for creating this title was not passed without a good deal of opposition and considerable augury of evil; but since it passed, it has been everywhere acquiesced in, and it is generally acknowledged that the Imperial title is the legitimate "outcome" of the visit paid in 1876 to India by the Prince of Wales, and meant to "testify the satisfaction felt by Her Majesty at the reception given to her son, and to emphasize at the same time the object of the visit."

The Queen has always been a ready patron o. talent, in whatever sphere it has shown itself, and has often summoned to her presence persons notable in literature, science, and art.

But it is not only as a Queen that Victoria has shown herself good; for she has been eminently throughout life a good daughter, a good sister, a

K 2

good wife, a good mother; and her children may well rise up and bless her.

The Prince of Wales and his brothers and sisters were all brought up by the Queen in a plain and simple way, and taught and trained to gain knowledge and to make themselves useful. Yes, as Miss Martineau writes, "the Queen's children have done real work with head and hands all their lives. After school hours, their play was another sort of work, the boys building a dairy with their own hands, and their sisters afterwards serving the dairy as real milkmaids. They have set their own cream and butter before the Queen; they have made ' stir-about' in Highland cabins ; and there is no member of the family who does not know that the moon is not made of green cheese."

Her Majesty's kindness of heart has shown itself on many occasions. She has been ever ready to help in any great or noble work, and to offer her sympathy with the sufferers from any calamity, whether it be from some destructive gale on our coasts, from fire or famine, or from an explosion in a mine. Her letters to Mr. Peabody on hearing of his munificent donation to the poor of London, and to Mrs. Abraham Lincoln on the assassination of her husband, the President of the United States, which were printed at full length in the papers at the time, were the genuine effusions of a tender and true-hearted woman, and did honour to her personally, and not only as a Queen. It was but the other day that, on reading the life of the humble

Scotch naturalist, Mr. Edward, Her Majesty expressed her wish that provision should be made for him in his old age, which has accordingly been done; and several widows and descendants of those who have made a name in literature have at different times during the Queen's reign, had cause to thank her for the provision which she has been the means of granting to them from the funds at her disposal.

The Queen has shone in all the different stages of her life; as a child, she was, as we have shown, engaging, affectionate, while she gave proof of talents of no common order, and possessed a thorough appreciation of the beauties of nature. Her early training served to bring out her talents and dispositions to the best advantage. As a wife and mother she has been a pattern to her subjects; and as a queen she has won a name which will be honoured as long as England herself lasts. Like Queen Elizabeth, she can boast, in the hours of her widowhood, that she is " married to her country." Loved and reverenced as she is by her subjects in all parts of the world, and even by thousands of those who do not own her sway, we may say, in the words of Burke, that should any insult, however small, be offered her, " a thousand swords would leap from their scabbards to avenge it." And this simply because Victoria reigns in the hearts of her people.

We must here bring, however, this slight sketch of the principal events of the Queen's life to a close; and, slight as it is, we feel sure that the facts recorded here will at the present time prove of some interest to our readers.

The late Earl of Shaftesbury observed :—" Let me remind you that there sits on the throne of these realms one who is a bright example to every one, even the poorest in her dominions. There can be nothing more beautiful or more simple than her domestic life, nothing more respectful to her husband, nothing more tender to her children ; but of this I am sure, that nothing would give her more delight than that we might to able to say 'After all, good as you are, happy and honourable as your life may be, your Majesty is no better than the rest of your subjects.' "

CHAPTER IX.

HER LATER LIFE.

"Break not, O royal heart, but still endure;
Break not, for thou art noble."
TENNYSON.

EARLY in the December of 1878, the Queen
received a second blow by the unexpected
death of the Princess Alice, when she
addressed to her subjects a most touching letter
which was published in the *Gazette*.

OSBORNE,
December, 26.

The Queen is anxious to take the earliest opportunity of expressing publicly her heartfelt thanks for the universal and most
touching sympathy shewn to her by all classes of her loyal and
faithful subjects on the present occasion, when it has pleased
God to call away from this world her dearly-beloved daughter,
the Princess Alice, Grand Duchess of Hesse. Overwhelmed
with grief at the loss of a dear child, who was a bright example
of loving tenderness, courageous devotion and self-sacrifice to
duty, it is most soothing to the Queen's feelings to see how
entirely her grief is shared by her people. The Queen's deeply-
afflicted son-in-law, the Grand Duke of Hesse, is also anxious

151

to make known his sincere gratitude for the kind feelings expressed towards himself and his dear children in their terrible
bereavement, and his gratification at the appreciation shown by
the people of England of the noble and endearing qualities of
her whom all now mourn. Seventeen years ago, at this very time,
when a similar bereavement crushed the Queen's happiness, and
this beloved and lamented daughter was her great comfort and
support, the nation evinced the same touching sympathy, as well
as when, in December, 1871, the Prince of Wales was at the
point of death. Such an exhibition of true and tender feeling
will ever remain engraven on the Queen's heart, and is the more
to be valued at this moment of great distress in the country,
which no one more deeply deplores than the Queen herself.

On this letter the *Standard* remarked :—

" The Message which the Queen, in her retirement at Osborne, has addressed to her people is
one that cannot fail to awaken fresh feelings of
sympathy with Her Majesty in her profound sorrow.
Whilst the nation has been observing one of the
chief Christian festivals the Queen has been ab-
sorbed in grief, and in comparative solitude has
mourned the loss of a beloved daughter.   The
greatness and severity of that loss it is not for us to
picture ; but we know how much it must have been
intensified by the sad associations connected with
it.   By the people the death of the Princess Alice
was felt as a personal bereavement.   In her they
had seen a noble type of true womanhood.   She
was—to quote the Queen's own words—' a bright
example of loving tenderness, courageous devotion,
and self-sacrifice to duty ; ' and it was because of
her tenderness, devotion, and self-abnegation that

she was so universally beloved. The anxiety which
was manifested by every class during her illness
was heartfelt, and the news of her death excited
emotions of deep and unaffected sorrow. Her excellent qualities had endeared her to the hearts of
the people, who were not slow to recognise her
womanly worth, and to offer their tribute of affectionate regard for her memory. The expression
of the public grief was as spontaneous as it was
sincere, and it moved the heart of the Queen. She
tells us, in her own touching language, how soothing has been its influence under the affliction with
which it has pleased Heaven to visit her, Herein
is seen the real nature of the ties that bind the
people of England to their beloved Sovereign.
Between the ruler and her subjects there is mutual
confidence and mutual friendship. The life of the
Queen is bound up in the happiness and well-being
of those whom she has been called upon to govern,
and these have ever warmly reciprocated the solicitude which her Majesty has shown on their behalf.
They know her as a Queen, and they have learned
to love her as a woman. In the hour of trial she
can freely unburden herself of her sorrow, because
she feels assured that it will be shared by the nation.
The letter penned by her on Thursday is one of
many which in the presence of a national calamity
she has addressed to her subjects, thus entering into
communion with their thoughts and feelings. The
well-chosen and expressive phrases employed by
Her Majesty reveal the workings of her mind and

enhance the value of her letter. That she should take this opportunity of saying how deeply she deplores the prevalence of so much distress in the country is what might have been expected from Her Majesty, who has always sought to identify the sufferings of the people with her own. Words of comfort are ever welcome, and while the poor will thank the Queen for her thoughtful remembrance of them in their distress, all classes will readily accept the assurance of Her Majesty that the ' true and tender feeling' called forth by the recent mournful event will ever remain engraved upon her heart."

In 1879 Her Majesty again visited the sunny south, occupying the Italian villa of Mr. C. Henfrey, at Baveno, for nearly a month. During this visit, the Queen walked about everywhere, saw everything that was to be seen and went shopping in the streets of Baveno, attended by Lady Churchill. On one occasion an awkward shop-boy brought down upon her head a quantity of carved wood which was lying on a shelf; but the Queen laughed good-naturedly at the accident.

In the April of 1880 the Queen accompanied by H.R.H. Prince and Princess of Wales and Princess Beatrice, attended the confirmation of the Princesses Elizabeth and Victoria, children of her daughter the Princess Alice, at Darmstadt.

In the December of 1882 Her Majesty paid another visit to the City in order to open formally the new Courts of Law, known technically as the

Palace of Justice, which had been erected by
Mr. G. E. Street, at the City end of the Strand,
close to Temple Bar.   On this occasion she raised
her Chancellor, Lord Selborne, as the head of the
legal profession, to an Earldom.

For the next two years the Queen rarely appeared
in public, though she held one or two Drawing
Rooms at Buckingham Palace.   In the year 1886
Her subjects were delighted to learn that Her
Majesty had made up her mind to take a part in
one or two public ceremonies, which it may be
hoped had the effect of weaning her back, to some
extent at least, from that self-imposed retirement,
which they began to fear had become so habitual
as to prove a second nature.   In the May of that
year she travelled from Windsor to Paddington,
and drove across Hyde Park to South Kensington
in order to open the Colonial and Indian Exhibition.
A few weeks later she made a journey to Liverpool to
inaugurate a great Exhibition there ; and in August
she paid a state visit to Edinburgh, and inspected
the International Exhibition in that city.   She
stayed two days in her ancient palace of Holyrood,
under King Arthur's Seat, where she was attended
by the Royal Archers of Scotland as her body-
guard, under their captain, the Marquis of Lothian,
whom she visited at his private residence near
Jedburgh, as well as the Duke of Buccleuch at
Dalkeith.   On the third day she continued her
journey northwards to her favourite home at
Balmoral.

Queen Victoria, though descended from our Norman and Plantagenet kings, has in her the blood of no
later Stuart sovereign than James I.; and as a nation
we may perhaps congratulate ourselves that she does
not reckon Henry VIII. among her forefathers, or
Queen Elizabeth as an ancestress.   Though she is
of Guelphic and Brunswick descent, yet in her
centre the lines of our Saxon sovereigns and of
the ancient kings of Scotland, so that she has
every claim to the throne that birth can give.

We close this memoir, making our own the
prayer of the Poet Laureate:

> " May she rule us long.
> And leave us rulers of her blood
> As noble till the latest day.
> May children of our children say,
> She wrought her people lasting good ;
>
> Her court was pure ; her life serene ;
> God gave her peace ; her land reposed ;
> A thousand claims to reverence closed
> In her as mother, wife, and queen."

Our National Anthem, " God save the Queen,"
is known to every English child, and is sung at all
public gatherings right heartily. Of late it has
been translated into several of the native tongues
of India, and the dark children in almost every
native school now sing it with all but equal
pleasure. To one verse of it, however, exception
has been taken—" Confound their politics, frustrate
their knavish tricks."—These words may have
been justified a century and a-half ago, when the
throne hung in the balance between the House of

Brunswick and the exiled Stuarts; but now most
persons feel them to be out of place, when sung in
churches. At all events they strike a wrong chord;
accordingly a Minor Canon of Westminster, the
Rev. F. Harford, has suggested another version,
which we venture to print here, as appropriate to
Her Majesty's Jubilee; premising that stanzas 3 and
4 are, of course, optional, and meant to be used
only on special occasions.

I.

GOD save our Gracious Queen;
Long live our Noble Queen:
   GOD SAVE THE QUEEN.
Send Her victorious,
Happy and glorious,
Long to reign over us;
   GOD SAVE THE QUEEN.

II.

For Her Majesty's Armies, in times of Peace or War.

O LORD, Our GOD! arise;
Scatter Her Enemies,
   And make them fall.
Bless Thou the brave that fight—
Sworn to defend Her Right.
Bending we own Thy Might.
   GOD save us all.

III.

Or this against Sedition.

O LORD, Our GOD! arise;
Scatter Her enemies,
   And make them fall.
Break Thou Rebellion's wings:
Smite when dark Treason springs.
Almighty KING of Kings,
   RULER of all!

IV.

Or this in time of Pestilence.

O LORD, Our GOD! arise ;
Help, while Destruction flies
   Swift o'er us all !
Stay Thine afflicting Hand :
Heal Thou our stricken Land.
FATHER! in grief we stand.
   On Thee we call.

V.

Thy choicest gifts in store
Still on VICTORIA pour—
   Health, Peace, and Fame.
Young faces year by year
Rising Her heart to cheer,
Glad voices, far and near,
   Blessing Her Name.

VI.

Saved from each traitor's arm,—
Thou, LORD, Her Shield from harm
   Ever hast been.
Angels around Her way
Watch, while by night and day
Millions with fervour pray,—
   "GOD SAVE THE QUEEN."

AN EARLY INSTANCE OF THE QUEEN'S CLEMENCY.

From " Sketches and Anecdotes of Her Majesty the Queen."

It is related that during the first few days of the reign of Queen Victoria, then a girl between nineteen and twenty years of age, some sentences of a court-martial were presented for her signature. One was death for desertion—a soldier was condemned to be shot, and his warrant presented to the Queen for her signature. She read it, paused, and looked up to the officer who had laid it before her, and said :—

"Have you nothing to say in behalf of this man ?"

"Nothing; he has deserted three times," said the officer.

"Think again, your grace," was her reply.

"And," said the gallant veteran, as he related the circumstance to his friends (for it was none other than the Duke of Wellington), "seeing Her Majesty so earnest about it, I said, he is certainly a bad *soldier*, but there was somebody who spoke as

to his good character, and he may be a good *man*
for aught I know to the contrary."

" Oh ! thank you a thousand times ! " exclaimed
the youthful Queen, and hastily writing *Pardoned*
in large letters on the fatal page, she sent it across
the table with a hand trembling with eagerness and
beautiful emotion.

THE QUEEN AND IRISH OUTRAGES.

The following letter, written by command of the
Queen to Lord Aberdare, President of the Royal
Society for the Prevention of Cruelty to Animals,
has just been published :—" Would it be possible
for the Royal Society for the Prevention of Cruelty
to Animals to take any steps with regard to the
houghing of cattle and other horrible practices on
dumb animals which are occurring so frequently
in Ireland ? This is no political question, and
some of the extreme so-called Nationalist papers
in Ireland condemn these cruelties as warmly as
the loyal journals. The Queen is most anxious
that every endeavour should be used to put a stop
to these cruelties, and has therefore commanded
me to ask if the aid of the Society, of which you
are President, can be granted, with the view of
preventing a recurrence of these crimes." The
Committee, it appears, had already anticipated the
Queen's wishes by sending a circular on the subject
to all its branches in Ireland ; and Lord Aberdare
replied that the Society can only appeal to the
moral sense of the people against such outrages.

THE QUEEN'S VISIT TO OLD PEOPLE AT BALMORAL.

From " A Journal of Our Life in the Highlands."

"Mrs. P. Farquharson walked round with us to some of the cottages to show me where the poor people lived, and to tell them who I was. Before we went into any we met an old woman, who Mrs. Farquharson said, was very poor, eighty-eight years of age. I gave her a warm petticoat, and the tears rolled down her old cheeks, and she shook my hands, and prayed God to bless me. It was very touching.

"I went into an old cabin of Old Kitty Kear's, who is eighty-six years old, quite erect, and who welcomed us with a great air of dignity. She sat down and spun. I gave her also a warm petticoat. She said, 'May the Lord ever attend ye an l yours, here and hereafter; and may the Lord be a guide to ye and keep ye from all harm.' She was quite surprised at Vicky's (Princess Royal) height. Great interest is taken in her. We went on to a cottage to visit the old Widow Symons, who is past 'fourscore,' with a nice rosy face, but was bent quite double, she was most friendly, shaking hands with us all, asking which was me, and re-peating many kind blessings. ' May the Lord attend ye with mirth and with joy; may He ever be with ye in this world, and when ye leave it.' To Vicky, when told she was going to be married, she said, ' May the Lord be a guide to ye in your

L

future, and may every happiness attend ye.' She
was very talkative, and when I said I hoped to see
her again, she expressed an expectation that 'she
should be called any day,' and so did Kitty Kear.

"We went into three other cottages; to Mrs.
Symons's (daughter-in-law to the old widow living
next door), who had an unwell boy; then across a
little tarn to another old woman's; and afterwards
peeped into Blair, the fiddler's. We drove back
again to visit old Mrs. Grant, who is so tidy and
clean, and to whom I gave a dress and handkerchief.
She said, 'You're too kind to me; you're o'er kind
to me; ye give me more every year, and I get older
every year.' After talking some time with me, she
said, 'I am happy to see you looking so nice.' She
had tears in her eyes, and, speaking of Vicky's
going, said, 'I'm very sorry, and I think she is
sorry hersel''; and having said she feared she would
not see her (the Princess) again, said, 'I'm very
sorry I said that, but I mean no harm; I always
say what I think, not what is fut' (fit). 'Dear old
lady, she is such a pleasant person.'

"Really the affection of these good people, who
are so hearty and so happy to see you, taking
interest in everything, is very touching and gratifying."

THE QUEEN AND HER LIBRARIAN.

"Mr. Woodward," observed Her Majesty one day,
when she paid a visit to the Royal Library at

Windsor, to enquire how he was getting on with the task of arranging some part of the many tons of MS. letters of the Stuarts, which were under the charge of her librarian, "you must know that I take a great interest in the Stuarts; in fact I am a devoted and enthusiastic admirer of that house." "And I, madam,". was his courtier-like reply, " may hope to be pardoned for saying that I am a devoted admirer of the House of Hanover." The Queen was much amused at Mr. Woodward's ready wit.

THE QUEEN AND THE SPITALFIELDS BOY.

On Her Majesty's visit to the London Hospital, she spoke to a boy, eight years of age, who had his leg broken by having been run over. As soon as he went home to Spitalfields, the child wrote, of his own accord, and without his father's or mother's knowledge, a letter to the Queen. He bought a stamp, and posted it. It bore no other address than the words " Lady Queen Victoria." It reached the Queen's hand and eye, and she discerned that it was simple and genuine in its childlike gratitude, and on due inquiry it has been found that it was the boy's own act. Her Majesty has sent a kind gift of £3, through her chaplain, the Rev. T. J. Rowsell. The parents have asked Mr. Rowsell to buy a Bible with some of the money to represent the gift.

INSTANCE OF THE QUEEN'S CLEMENCY.

From the " Hamilton U. C. Spectator."

A soldier named Darragh was tried in Ireland for
Fenianism; he was found guilty and sentenced to
be shot. The warrant was brought to the Queen
for signature; her consent was urgently solicited,
on the ground of the necessity of making an example. Her Majesty, whose attachment to the
soldiers of her army has always been proverbial, for
a long time refused, but at length was induced to
sign the warrant—though she burst into tears in
the act of doing so. Within an hour afterwards
she sent for the warrant again and tore it to pieces.
Without going into the question of whether Her
Majesty's clemency was wisely extended to a soldier
who had been false to his colours and his oath, this
additional proof of the Queen's humanity and kindness of heart will be appreciated by all her subjects,
and few will hesitate to say " God bless her " for it.

QUEEN VICTORIA SHOPPING AT BAVENO.

The Piedmontese *Gazette* says:—" The weather was most abominable, but Her Majesty sallied out on foot, notwithstanding, accompanied by Lady Churchill. The two ladies sheltered themselves as well as they could by keeping close to the walls of the houses of Baveno, and they turned in to make a visit to the pin and needle factory. In returning to the villa Clara they entered a shop where carved wood is sold. Just imagine the Queen of England and Empress of the Indies in a 'shop,' and speaking familiarly with a 'shopkeeper' like any ordinary tourist. Well, the poor Bavenian carver began by turning all his stock upside down to show it to the illustrious hostess of the Villa Clara. However, it so happened that his unhandy assistant let a ladder slip down, and a number of things on the upper steps fell to the ground in the upset. The Queen was standing beneath, and quite an avalanche of carved wood came pouring on her august head and shoulders, as well as on Lady Churchill's. Fortunately, neither lady was hurt. But you may judge what the consequences might have been had the goods been a little heavier. The poor shopkeeper was near fainting, and lost the use of his tongue for a few minutes. The Queen, however, only laughed heartily at the accident, and said jokingly to Lady Churchill as they went out that she supposed people would say it was one more attempt on à Sovereign's life ! "

THE QUEEN'S DEVOTION TO HER HUSBAND.

It was foreseen that the death of the Prince Consort would not be allowed to pass over without much gossip as to what was said here and there at this harrowing moment and at that. Fifty absurd stories of this sort, all "on excellent authority, I assure you," have got into circulation privately, and though they are willingly repeated from mouth to mouth, there are not many which anyone believes in enough to vouch for them publicly. The vicar of Bradford, however, has come forward as an exception. In proposing the health of Her Majesty, he said he would relate an anecdote which he had obtained from a private source which placed its authenticity beyond doubt. When Her Majesty was somewhat recovering from the overwhelming grief which the death of the Prince Consort excited in her bosom, she remarked to those around her:—"It is impossible for me to say how I loved and revered that man. If it had been my lot, I could have been content to walk barefoot through the world with him."

―――――

THE QUEEN'S MOTHERLY CARE FOR HER SUBJECTS.

In January, 1865, Her Majesty, through Sir C. Phipps, called the attention of the directors of the principal railways to the increasing number of accidents, expressing at the same time, her strong wish and warm hope that they would carefully, consider every means against these misfortunes, which, she added, with no little humour, "are not at all the necessary accompaniments of railway travelling." This letter was not dictated by any selfish motives, for whenever the Queen travels on railways all sorts of extraordinary precautions against accidents are taken.

THE QUEEN AND JENNY LIND.

From " Sketches and Anecdotes of the Queen."

When Jenny Lind first sang in private before the Queen, she was accompanied by the Queen's pianist, who, being connected with a rival theatre, in his playing disconcerted Mdlle. Lind exceedingly. This, the quick ear of Her Majesty, who is an excellent musician, instantly detected; and as Jenny stood up for the second, the Queen motioned the pianist aside, saying quietly, "I will accompany Mdlle. Lind," which she did to perfection. How perfectly does this little incident accord with the characteristics of the kindness, benevolence and tact for which Her Majesty is so remarkable !

THE QUEEN'S PROMISE TO A SCOTCH LASSIE.

" Several years ago," writes a correspondent of the *Aberdeen Free Press*, " Her Majesty on leaving her

Highland residence for the season, promised to
Jenny ———, daughter of a cotter in the vicinity,
to bring a toy to her next year. During the
interval some very important State affairs passed,
and the Queen was over in France on a visit to the
Emperor. The promise was all but forgotten on
one side, that of the Highland girl; not so on the
other, for on arriving at Balmoral next season, Her
Majesty presented the humble lassie with the
promised toy, remarking, 'See, I have not forgotten
you.' "

THE QUEEN AND "UNCLE TOM."

The presentation to Her Majesty, by special command, of the Rev. Josiah Henson occurred about
ten years ago at Windsor Castle. As previously
arranged, the negro patriarch was accompanied by
Mrs. Henson and by his friend, Mr. John Lobb.
The party reached the Castle at one p.m., and were
received by Sir T. M. Biddulph, K.C.B., who, after
introducing them to Major-General Ponsonby,
invited them to partake of luncheon. At three,
Her Majesty, accompanied by His Royal Highness
Prince Leopold and Her Royal Highness Princess
Beatrice appeared in the corridor leading to the
Oak room, attended by the Hon. Horatia Stopford
and the Countess of Erroll, Ladies in Waiting.
The Rev. Josiah Henson, " Uncle Tom," was then
presented to Her Majesty by Sir T. M. Biddulph.

Her Majesty expressed pleasurable surprise at the coloured clergyman's striking hale and hearty looks, considering his great age. He was born on June 15th 1789. Her Majesty was also pleased to say that for many years she had been well acquainted with his history, and to present him with her portrait. Mr. Henson thanked Her Majesty on his own behalf for the great honour conferred upon himself, as well as on behalf of his coloured brethren in Canada and other portions of Her Majesty's dominions, for her august protection when they were poor fugitive slaves, and for the unspeakable blessings they had at all times enjoyed under her rule. Mr. Lobb was then presented by Sir T. M. Biddulph to Her Majesty as the editor of Mr. Henson's "Autobiography," a copy of which had been graciously accepted by Her Majesty, who was pleased to say that she had read it with much interest and pleasure. At Her Majesty's gracious request the autographs of the Rev. Josiah Henson and Mr. J. Lobb, with the date of the birth of each, were then inscribed in Her Majesty's private album.

THE QUEEN'S PORTRAIT FOR THE PEOPLE.

From "Sketches and Anecdotes of the Queen."

The following anecdote of the Queen illustrates her good sense and real desire to promote the welfare of her subjects. She had agreed to have her photograph taken for the gratification of such

of her subjects as might desire to possess the
counterfeit presentment of their ruler. She presented herself in a plain black silk, without a
particle of ornament. The photographer ventured
to suggest that she should send for some jewels.
"No," said the Queen, "this photograph is to go
among my people, and I wish to do all in my
power to discourage extravagance." It is such
traits as these that have secured the Queen a high
place in the regard of the people.

THE QUEEN AND HER SPINNING WHEEL.
From the " Cincinnati Gazette."

Before leaving Germany, the Queen took a fancy
to spinning, and ordered a mechanic of Spitalfields
to make her a spinning wheel. He finished one
of such exquisite workmanship, that she ordered
one for each of her palaces and castles. The good
royal matron resumes the occupation of the simple
ladies of old and unaffected times ; and be sure
her example will not be lost on the fashionable
and bejewelled ladies of our age. The inclinations
and fancies of Queens dictate the fashion at the
spinning wheel as well as the Court toilet.

A CONFIDENTIAL SECRETARY TO THE QUEEN.

The *Court Journal* wrote thus in 1870, showing
the greatness of the great loss sustained by the

Queen in the death of the Prince Consort, who
for so many years had been her friend and
adviser, and had acted as her Secretary on many
occasions, " Wearing the white flower of a blame-
less life."—" There is no more difficult task for the
loyalty and devotion of the present Ministry than
to arrange for the future conduct of business
matters with the Queen.   Previous to her Majesty's
marriage, Lord Melbourne, with the concurrence of
the leaders of the great parties in the State, went
to the Palace every day and did the duty of confidential secretary.   Since her Majesty's accession to
the Empire of India, the public business of the
Crown has greatly increased.   We believe one of
the suggestions has been, in certain cases, to make
the signature of a Secretary of State sufficient—
countersigned, perhaps, by another Cabinet Minister
—but the chief object would be to find for the
Queen a confidential servant, such a one as was Sir
Herbert Taylor to William IV.   The real difficulty
of such an appointment is the political one, for he
must be one in whom a Liberal and a Conservative
Cabinet could have equal confidence ; for if with
every change of Ministry there were to be a
change in this office, the trouble and inconvenience
to the Queen would be enormous.   Possibly the
influence of the King of the Belgians among the
leading statesmen of the day might induce a perfect
accord as to the selection of a nobleman or gentleman for this important post."

THE QUEEN AND HER BALMORAL DEPENDANTS.

From the "Edinburgh Daily Review."

Of all the admirable traits in Her Majesty's personal character, none is more endearing than the interest she takes in her dependants, and her anxiety to promote their happiness.

A very touching instance of this has come to our notice. We do not need to say what sums would have been given by many proud millionaires of England for a place in St. George's Chapel at the great ceremony of the Prince of Wales's marriage. But the pleasure and honour for which these men must wish in vain was enjoyed by the humblest on the Highland estate at Balmoral. Her Majesty graciously invited the whole of her dependants there to be present at the marriage of her son, and ordered arrangements to be made for the conveyance to and from Windsor of as many persons as could possibly be spared from their duties upon the estate. They in their turn have evinced their affection for their Royal Mistress by many simple but pleasing expedients—such, for instance, as sending to many distant places chaplets and crowns of heather cut from the Prince's own forest at Braemar.

THE QUEEN'S FIRST COUNCIL.

Mr. Charles Greville's account of the Queen's performance of her lesson at her first Council has an

interest all its own. Lord Melbourne had suggested
to Her Majesty what she was to do, having first
learned it himself, and during the ceremony she
kept occasionally looking to him for instruction. She
went through it, however, "with perfect calmness
and self-possession, but at the same time with a
graceful modesty and propriety particularly interesting and ingratiating." So much so indeed,
that the Duke of Wellington—though the remark
sounds queer—said that "if she had been his own
daughter he could not have desired her to do it
better." The task must indeed have been a trying
one for a girl of "extreme youth and inexperience;"
nor can one wonder that, when she saw her two
elderly uncles on their knees before her, kissing
her hand and swearing allegiance, she should have
"blushed up to the eyes," Her Majesty has now
become, one would imagine, tolerably familiar with
the ceremonies appertaining to the holding of
Councils of all sorts, but it may be safely predicted
that she still looks back to the first Council as a
thing of awe and nervousness never to be forgotten.

THE QUEEN AND THE DUCHESS'S WATCH.

When Queen Victoria was many years younger
than she is now, she was inclined to be very exact
in the way of business, and more especially in the
way of promptness to appointed times and places.
Seven years a queen; four years a wife; and three

years a mother, she felt probably a. more weighty
dignity resting upon her than she has felt since.
And yet, no crust of dignity or royal station could
ever entirely shut out her innate goodness of heart.
At the time of which we speak the Duchess of
Sutherland held the office of Mistress of the
Robes to the Queen, and on public occasions her
position was very near to the royal person, and
deemed of great importance. A day and an hour
had been appointed for a certain public ceremony
in which the Queen was to take part. The hour
had arrived, and of all the Court the Duchess alone
was absent, and her absence retarded the departure.
The Queen gave vent more than once to her
impatience, and at length, just as she was about to
enter her carriage without her first lady of honour
the Duchess, in breathless haste, made her appearance, stammering some faint words of excuse.
"My dear Duchess," said the Queen, smiling, "I
think you must have a bad watch." And as she
thus spoke she unloosed from her neck the chain
of a magnificent watch which she herself wore,
and passed it around the neck of the Duchess.
Though given as a present, the lesson conveyed
with it made a deep and lively impression. The
proud Duchess changed colour, and a tear, which
she could not repress, fell upon her cheek. Next
day, she tendered her resignation, but it was not
accepted. It is said that ever afterwards she was, if
anything, more punctual than the Queen herself.

THE QUEEN AND A QUESTION OF GRAMMAR.

One consequence of the length to which the exceptionally prosperous reign of her Majesty has extended, has been to give to anecdotes and gossip about the first portion of it, all the characteristics of history. The dispute as related in the "Greville Memoirs," between Sir Robert Peel and Lord Brougham as to the use of the word "amelioration" in her first "Queen's Speech," has quite an anti-quarian interest. "Amelioration," said Brougham, "that is not English; you might, perhaps, say 'melioration,' but 'improvement' is the proper word." "Oh!" replied Peel, "I see no harm in the word." "You object to the sentiment," said Brougham, "I object to the grammar." "No," said Peel, "I don't object to the sentiment." "Well, then, she pledges herself to the policy of *our* Government," was Brougham's answer.

THE QUEEN AND RELIGIOUS PERSECUTION.

From an anonymous pamphlet entitled "The Queen,"
published by Partridge & Co.

It was a kindly thought of Queen Victoria, when the draft treaty arranging for peace and commerce between England and Madagascar was sent out, to write on the margin, "Queen Victoria asks as a personal favour to herself, that the Queen of Madagascar will allow no persecution of Christians."

The word spoken in due season was not without its effect, for in the treaty sent back and signed a short time afterwards, the words occur, " In accordance .with the wish of Queen Victoria, the Queen of Madagascar engages that there shall be no persecution of the Christians in Madagascar."

THE QUEEN AND THE SICK CHILD.

An instance of the Queen's regard for little folks occurred during her visit to the London Hospital in 1876, when a little sick girl in the children's ward cried out to the nurse, " Please do let me see the Queen; I shall be quite better if I see the Queen." This request was communicated to the Rev. Mr. Rowsell, Her Majesty's Chaplain, who told the Queen. Immediately Her Majesty did that which pleased her people not a little when the tale was told. She asked to be taken to the bedside of the child, and there spoke loving words of tenderness and sympathy, which were doubtless far more really healing in their effect, than the "royal touch" which her ancestors used to dispense in a superstitious age.

THE QUEEN AND HER TUTOR.

The late Bishop (Davys) of Peterborough, a prelate, whose unobtrusive character caused him to be little known, except among his own people,

was tutor to the Queen from 1823 to 1837, and
some touching words spoken " with considerable
emotion " by him on moving an address of condolence to the Queen (written by himself), may be
interesting to our readers :—" Perhaps no one
living knew more of Her Majesty's private character than himself, and he knew what deep and
tender feelings she had. From a letter he had
received the previous day, in reply to a letter of
condolence which he had written and had directed
to Her Majesty's private secretary, they might
judge how their address was likely to be received,
because the Queen was the same both in public and
in private as to her feelings. The answer was
written by Lady Augusta Bruce, lady in waiting
upon the Queen, and, he had no doubt, expressed
Her Majesty's own sentiments. ' I have received
the Queen's commands,' says the writer, 'to convey
Her Majesty's warm acknowledgments of the
feeling letter of sympathy addressed to her.' And
the letter proceeded to say, that at this terrible
moment, if anything could assuage her overwhelming grief, it was the deep share in that grief taken
by the whole nation, and the expression of the
feelings of those whose prayers were rising continually to Heaven for Her Majesty and for her
fatherless children. They were very soothing and
welcome to the Queen's bleeding heart. To the
continual prayers of the people had already been
vouchsafed some answer from Heaven in the

M

resignation and patience granted to the Queen, and in the preservation of Her Majesty's health. 'Weak and exhausted,' said the writer in conclusion, 'the Queen is; but there is no violent reaction from the shock, and nothing to cause anxiety or alarm.' This last sentence must be very gratifying to them all. They knew Her Majesty's noble heart, and had every reason to fear that the shock would indeed be great. It had been great, but, thank God, 'there is nothing to cause anxiety or alarm.'"

THE QUEEN AS A CATECHIST.

"Queen Victoria, when at home," writes a Canadian paper, the *Hamilton Spectator*, "regularly teaches a Sunday School and Bible Class for the benefit of those residing in the palace and its vicinity. The Archdeacon of London on one occasion was cate-chising the young princes, and, being surprised at the accuracy of their answers, said to the youngest prince, 'Your governess deserves great credit for instructing you so thoroughly in the Catechism,' 'Oh! but it is mamma who teaches us the Catechism.'"

THE QUEEN AND HER ARAB HORSES.
From the "Globe."

Our readers will remember that some years ago Her Majesty made a present to Mr. Batty, the

lessee of Astley's Theatre, of two out of several
Arabian horses sent to the Queen by the Emperor
of Morocco, that her subjects might have the
gratification of seeing pure specimens of this
renowned breed of animals. They were two entire
horses, spotlessly white in colour, perfect in sym-
metry, pure in blood, standing about 14 hands
2 inches in height, and rising one four and the
other five years old. The animals were committed
to the care of experienced breakers and trainers,
under the immediate eye and superintendence of
Mr. Batty himself, and both have become perfectly
docile, and thoroughly obedient to the whip and
rein, whether in single or double harness; and in
the course of two or three weeks, such is their
docility and intelligence, that they are expected to
be sufficiently well up in their parts and the business of the stage, to make their *début* upon the
boards, where so many of their kindred and clime
long sustained a distinguished reputation, and
attracted crowded audiences. Her Majesty also
presented Mr. Batty with a mare of the same breed
and colour, but slightly freckled with black spots.
She is a beautiful animal, with a broad chest, much
bottom, and a particularly graceful head and sloping
back. She is considerably older than the horses,
but from her build and temper she is not unlikely
to verify the old adage that "the grey mare is the
better horse." Mr. Batty is, as he well may be,
proud of Her Majesty's present, and bestows all

the care and skill he possibly can to make their training worthy of their blood, and their performances acceptable to the Royal donor and her loyal subjects.

___

THE QUEEN AND HER DOMESTIC GRIEFS.
From "London," December, 1878.

Her Majesty has hitherto been singularly fortunate, with one melancholy exception, in her family relations. Putting her widowhood out of question, she has known no bereavement of the nearest and bitterest kind. There are probably few mothers who reach the age of three-score years and who, out of a numerous family, have not to lament the loss of a single member. Until the death of the Princess Alice, Her Majesty was in this position, and though she had lost descendants in the second generation, her own family circle remained as unbroken as it was when the Prince Consort left it.

It is a just boast of the present Royal Family that they are before all things an united family. The unfortunate and almost inevitable jealousies and dissensions which in other countries and other times have separated parents from children and brethren from brethren have had no parallel in the present English Court. This family unity has been (and we certainly need not blush to avow it before foreigners) no slight factor in the production of the sentiments of loyalty and respect with

which all Englishmen worthy of the name now
regard the Throne. But family affection has, if
only by paradox, its disadvantages. The inevitable
losses and separations are harder to bear, harder to
get over, harder to compensate. The threefold
cord is not quickly broken in one way, but in
another it yields to irresistible force, and the wrench
is greater than if the bond had been slight. It is
impossible, too, but that the blow should be felt
more heavily from the moment of its occurrence at
the very time when the Queen is accustomed to
celebrate the anniversary of another and still
greater loss. Yet even this accident has its
consolations. The anniversary of the Prince
Consort's death has collected round Her Majesty
not a few of those surviving children of hers who
might otherwise not have been at hand. They are
her best and most suitable consolers, and it is not
for us to attempt the commonplaces of consolation
in addition to theirs. But there is one consolation
which has sometimes been held to be the most
effective of all, and which every one of Her
Majesty's subjects can give, and we are certain does
give her. This is the consolation of sympathy,
which is as valid—perhaps more valid—from beggar
as from king, from stranger as from familiar friend.
There have been monarchs who were indifferent to
this sympathy on the part of their subjects; there
have unfortunately been others to whom their
subjects had no thought of offering it. Her

Majesty is in happier case. Her subjects on this
and all similar occasions sympathise heartily with
her, and she is known to be as heartily glad to
receive their sympathy."

THE QUEEN AS SHE IS.

From the " Whitehall Review," June 24th, 1880.

" Forty-three years ago last Sunday a girl of
eighteen was aroused from her sleep at five o'clock
on a bright summer morning by the Archbishop
of Canterbury and Lord Conyngham. In dressing-
gown and slippers, with her long hair flowing in
disorder over her shoulders, she went downstairs to
hear the momentous tidings that she, Princess
Victoria, was Queen of England. 'She burst into
a flood of tears,' says the Archbishop, 'and,
trembling and faint, fell down on her knees, and
entreated me to join with her in a prayer to
Heaven for grace to discharge the duties thus
placed upon her.' Those of us who see the
Queen at Windsor next Sunday—Coronation Day
—will be disposed to take a retrospective glance
over the interval; but of outward demonstration,
save the firing of guns and the joyous peal from
the bells of many steeples, there will be nothing to
mark the anniversary. Yet we might for once
have had a national *fete* this year, decked our
streets with flags and triumphal arches, as was

wont to be done in the days that are gone, by
many of our loyal municipalities, who regarded
the anniversary of the Coronation as their holiday
par excellence. The Government of the day might
well have consulted Her Majesty's feelings on the
subject of a great *fête* to be celebrated by the
whole nation, the echoes of which would have
gone far and wide, for it is seldom in the history of
any country that the monarch happily survives to
reign over her subjects for hard upon half a
century. Probably the Queen, all diffident as we
know her to be, would shrink from such a manifesta-
tion of the popular feeling ; for, assured as she is
of the loyal love of her people, she does not seek
those outward and visible signs of respect which
seem inseparable from the careers of many foreign
sovereigns. The fact is that the Queen, whose
stately figure is too well known to need any
portraiture in words, is a thorough Englishwoman
in her intense love of home. When she paid her
first visit to Balmoral she jotted down in her diary :
'It is so calm and solitary, and the pure mountain
air so refreshing, it does one good as one gazes
around. All seems to breathe freedom and peace,
and to make one forget the world and its turmoils.'
And later, showing that her first feelings were
confirmed by experience, the Queen says : 'Every
year my heart becomes more fixed in this dear
Paradise, and so much more now that all has
become my dear Albert's own creation, own work,

own building, own laying out, just as at Osborne;
and his great taste and the impress of his dear
hand have been stamped upon it everywhere.'

"As a child the Queen was very little at Windsor,
and Balmoral and Osborne were as yet unbuilt.
The chief homes of her childhood were the dismal
old palace at Kensington, the secluded groves of
Claremont, and Norris Castle, near Cowes. She
also spent several months at a time at Ramsgate,
St. Leonard's, Broadstairs, and Tunbridge Wells, at
each of which places she left behind her pleasant
memories which have not yet quite died out.

"There can be no doubt that in the early part of
her reign the Queen was strongly attached to the
Whigs, and that she looked up for advice in almost
everything to her uncle Sussex and old Lord
Melbourne, who happened to be First Lord of the
Treasury; and when, at the end of four years, Peel
and the Conservatives came into power, it was not
at once that she took kindly to her new advisers.
Plenty of proofs of this might be found in the
journal of the Duke of Wellington's friend and
correspondent, Mr. Raikes. I need not say that
the Queen speaks German as fluently as English;
and German is still, as it was in the Prince
Consort's time, talked in her own domestic circle.
French is Her Majesty's language in writing or
speaking to diplomatists; but in the privacy of
Osborne and Balmoral it is, and has always been,
the *Deutsche Sprache.*

"There is one thing to which, as I well know, the Queen has the most unconquerable aversion, that is, for any lady of her Court to betray the least of its secrets. I do not, of course, allude to important State secrets, but to such subjects of gossip as her daily mode of life—her hours of rising, going to bed, and so forth. We are occasionally let into a few of these in the book on her Highland life; but generally speaking, I fancy that she holds with the emperor mentioned by Tacitus when he says, '*Majestati major ex longinquo reverentia.*'

"Women generally like, albeit in middle life, to feel some strong arm by their side on which to lean for counsel and advice even in little things. Before she was married the Queen's friend was Lord Melbourne; as a wife, she found her friend, as she ought, in her husband. And now, in her maturer years, she constantly consults in the lesser matters of everyday life two intimate friends—her chaplains, Dean Stanley and the Dean of Windsor, the latter of whom, if I mistake not, is, in theory, the 'confessor' of the Royal Household at Windsor.

"The Queen is every inch a woman in her correspondence. I do not wish to read nicer short letters than those which, as Princess Victoria, she wrote to Sir John Conroy nearly forty years ago, whilst on her tour in the Midlands and in North Wales with her mother—letters in which she orders bracelets, watches, rings, and other presents for those who made her tour agreeable at the various houses

which she visited. And ten or twelve years later I
was delighted with a right womanly note which she
addressed to the Duchess of Gloucester, full of
italics and notes of admiration, thanking her
'dearest aunt' for the 'pretty presents which she
has lately sent to dear little Bertie and Vic.' In
another letter the Queen shows the maternal
element strongly ; while staying at Inverary Castle
with the Duke of Argyll some thirty years ago, she
writes : ' Outside the great gate stood the Marquis
of Lorne, just two years old, a dear, white, fat little
fellow, with reddish hair, but very delicate features :
like both his father and his mother ; he is such a
merry independent little child. He had on a black
velvet dress and jacket with a " sporran," a scarf,
and a Highland bonnet.' Little, indeed, could she
then have imagined that the merry and chubby
child would one day be her son-in-law. And, then,
as to the art of saying or writing the right thing
in occasions of deep grief and affliction—here I
think the Queen of England shines out a true
woman ; at all events few manifestoes could have
gone so straight to the hearts of all England as the
letters which she addressed to her people on the
deaths of the Prince Consort and the Princess Alice,
and on the scarcely-expected recovery of the Prince
of Wales.

"Extremely fond of art, too, is the Queen, and
when she is at Windsor she does not often let a
month pass by without taking a peep into the

Royal Library, which contains, besides the books accessible to visitors, one of the finest collections of engravings and specimens of the Old Masters, both English and foreign. There are drawers and drawers full of these, all carefully catalogued and indexed. But what she prides herself most upon is her unrivalled collection of miniatures, a few only of which have seen the light at various loan exhibitions; and she is accustomed to boast, with a laugh, that in this respect she has only one rival in Great Britain, and that is his Scottish Majesty, the Duke of Buccleuch. Her Majesty shows her love of art in another way. From a child she was always fond of drawing, and sketched well from nature. We have many bold and characteristic sketches from her pencil in " Our Life in the Highlands "; and I have seen a pencil sketch of the front of Claremont, in very sharp perspective, drawn by her from nature whilst still a Princess, but well worthy of being hung at the " Black and White " exhibition for its boldness and freedom. That at sixty Her Majesty's hand has not lost its cunning may be inferred from the fact that she went out daily sketching the mountain scenery round Baveno last year.

" The Queen is, by the confession of more than one of her Prime Ministers, an excellent business woman. One of them, indeed, describes her as not only wonderfully conversant with State business, even before her marriage, but also as taking

an 'all-absorbing interest' in it. 'When a mes-
senger's box is brought down to the Castle,' he
writes, 'her countenance, which is naturally
serious, brightens up immediately. She reads all
the despatches, and makes her comments; and is
so engrossed by this one idea that she never enters
into the light gossiping conversation to which
most young women are addicted.' I have seen
several despatches in her handwriting, addressed to
Lord John Russell, Lord Melbourne, and Lord
Aberdeen, with her signature, 'The Queen,' in
the corner, after the manner of a frank. Whenever
she used this superscription there was some remark
or other endorsed on the paper within. These
boxes are always sent backwards and forwards
between the Queen and her Ministers by royal
messengers, each of whom has a duplicate key.

"It would be possible, of course, to give many
incidents and recollections which would be read
with thrilling interest by a great number of people;
but I do not forget that I am writing of my Sovereign, and that the laws of good taste restrain the
pen. It has fallen to my lot to see Her Majesty
under a great variety of circumstances. What has
struck me most is her consummate grace of manner,
her unaffectedness, her great dignity, but above
and beyond all these her supreme *pity* for the grief-
stricken and the afflicted, whether they be highly
or lowly-born. There is a gloriously-pathetic side
to the Queen's character which shows itself in

many ways. I thought it attained its most poetic point when I saw the Mother of England lay her wreath on the coffin of the Hope of France."

THE QUEEN'S FAVOURITE SONGS.
From the "Pall Mall Gazette."

What are the favourite songs of the Queen ? The question suggests itself from the list which appears in the papers :—

"Nature's Praise."	"Hail to the Chief."
"Ye Banks and Braes."	"Wae's me for Prince Charlie."
"The Silent Land."	"When Evening Twilight."
"I am going to my lonely bed."	"Praise of Spring."
"Jack and Jill."	"Homeward,"

"In this hour of softened splendour."
"Break, break, on thy cold grey stones."

These are the songs which were sung to the Queen by the Aberdeen Madrigal Choir on Tuesday. Most of these ballads treat of melancholy subjects. Does the Queen select her own programme ?

THE QUEEN AND FREE LIBRARIES.

The following letter has been received by a gentleman of Wolverhampton, who had sent to the Queen a description of an invention to facilitate the issue of books at the Wolverhampton Free

Library, and also a statement respecting the library
since its formation :—

"Buckingham Palace, Oct. 1873.

"Sir,—I am desired to acknowledge your letter to the Queen,
with a statement relative to Mr. John Elliott's invention for
issuing books, and a statement of the Wolverhampton Free
Library. I am to say that her Majesty is always gratified at
hearing of any plans by which additional facilities and induce-
ments are afforded to the working classes to make use of public
libraries, and her Majesty is pleased to know that in so thickly
populated a district as that lying around Wolverhampton such
facilities exist, and are apparently so much appreciated by the
class for whom the libraries have been established.—I have the
honour to be, Sir, your obedient Servant.

"T. M. BIDDULPH.
"Mr. W. H. Darkin."

THE NEW "QUEEN'S HEADS."

The new postage stamp has been in circulation for
some time, but it cannot be said that the remarks
it elicits are very complimentary to the artist who
designed it, or to Her Majesty, whose image it
presumably bears. It was never pretended that
the "Queen's Head" bore any likeness to the head
of the Queen—even at the date of her coronation ;
and the one now presented to the public in the
fresh issue of postage stamps, is made still more
unlike by the surroundings. It is smaller and more
juvenile-like, giving one the impression that the
older she grows the younger she gets.

LETTER FROM THE PRINCE OF WALES.

The following is the text of the letter addressed by H.R.H. the Prince of Wales to the Lord Mayor of London, in which the suggestion of the foundation of a Colonial Institute as a memorial of the Queen's Jubilee first took shape and form :—

"Marlborough House, Pall Mall, S.W.
"Dear Lord Mayor,   "Sept. 13, 1886.

"My attention has been frequently called to the general anxiety that is felt to commemorate in some special manner the approaching Jubilee of Her Majesty's reign. It appears to me that no more suitable memorial could be suggested than an institute which should represent the arts, manufactures and commerce of the Queen's Colonial and Indian Empire. Such an institution would, it seems to me, be singularly appropriate to the occasion, for it would illustrate the progress already made during Her Majesty's reign in the Colonial and Indian Dominions, while it would record year by year the development of the Empire in the arts of civilisation. It would thus be deeply interesting to Her Majesty's subjects, both within and beyond these islands, and would tend to stimulate emigration to those British territories where it is required, to expand the trade between the different British communities, and to draw closer the bonds which unite the Empire. It would be at once a museum, an exhibition, and the proper locality for the discus-

sion of Colonial and Indian subjects. That public
attention has already been forcibly directed to
these questions is sufficiently proved by the remarkable success which is attending the Colonial
and Indian Exhibition at South Kensington, and I
confidently anticipate that arrangements may be
made whereby the more important collections which
have so largely contributed to this success, will be
placed at the disposal of the institution. I have
much satisfaction in addressing this letter to your
Lordship as chief magistrate of the capital of the
Empire, and to invite your co-operation in the
formation of this Imperial Institute of the Colonies
and India, as the memorial of Her Majesty's
Jubilee by her subjects. Should your Lordship
concur in this proposal, and be willing to open a
fund at the Mansion House, I would suggest that
the contributions received be vested in a body of
trustees, whom the Sovereign would be asked to
nominate; and I would further suggest that the
institution should be under the permanent presi-
dency of the Heir Apparent to the Throne.—I
remain, dear Lord Mayor, yours truly,

"ALBERT EDWARD P.

" The Right Hon. the Lord Mayor."

DIPROSE, BATEMAN & Co., Printers, Sheffield Street,
Lincoln's Inn Fields.

CPSIA information can be obtained
at www.ICGtesting.com
Printed in the USA
BVHW061713040419
544635BV00017B/281/P